First World War
and Army of Occupation
War Diary
France, Belgium and Germany

32 DIVISION
97 Infantry Brigade
Highland Light Infantry
16th (Service) Battalion (2nd Glasgow)
23 November 1915 - 30 April 1918

WO95/2403/2

The Naval & Military Press Ltd
www.nmarchive.com
Published in association with The National Archives

Published by

The Naval & Military Press Ltd

Unit 10 Ridgewood Industrial Park,
Uckfield, East Sussex,
TN22 5QE England
Tel: +44 (0) 1825 749494

www.naval-military-press.com

www.nmarchive.com

This diary has been reprinted in facsimile from the original. Any imperfections are inevitably reproduced and the quality may fall short of modern type and cartographic standards.

© Crown Copyright
Images reproduced by permission of The National Archives, London, England, 2015.

Contents

Document type	Place/Title	Date From	Date To
Heading	WO95/2403-2 97 Inf Bde 16 Btn HLI		
Heading	32nd Division 97th Infy Bde 16th Bn High'D Lt Infy Nov 1915-1918 Feb Pioneers From March 1918 Same Div To 32 Div Troop		
Heading	War Diary of 16th (Service) Battalion the Highland Light Infantry From 23rd November 1915 to 31st December 1915 Volume II		
Miscellaneous			
Miscellaneous	Novbr & Dec. 1915 32nd 16th H.L.I. Vol 11 2.3		
War Diary	Codford	23/11/1915	23/11/1915
War Diary	Boulogne	23/11/1915	25/11/1915
War Diary	Longpre	25/11/1915	25/11/1915
War Diary	Surcamps and Vauchelles	26/11/1915	27/11/1915
War Diary	St Vast En Chaussee	28/11/1915	28/11/1915
War Diary	Pierregot	29/11/1915	01/12/1915
War Diary	Senlis and Martinsart	02/12/1915	07/12/1915
War Diary	Sector G 3	08/12/1915	11/12/1915
War Diary	Senlis and Martinsart	12/12/1915	12/12/1915
War Diary	Pierregot	13/12/1915	22/12/1915
War Diary	Martinsart	23/12/1915	23/12/1915
War Diary	F2 Sector	24/12/1915	27/12/1915
War Diary	Aveluy	28/12/1915	31/12/1915
Miscellaneous	16th (Service) Battalion H.L.I. Appendix I		
Heading	War Diary of 16 (Service) Battalion the Highland Light Infantry From 1st January 1916 to 31st January 1916 Volume III		
Miscellaneous			
War Diary	F2 Sector	01/01/1916	07/01/1916
War Diary	Bouzincourt and Aveluy	08/01/1916	14/01/1916
War Diary	F2 Sector	15/01/1916	27/01/1916
War Diary	Aveluy	28/01/1916	28/01/1916
War Diary	F2 Sector	29/01/1916	31/01/1916
Heading	32 16th H.L.I. Vol 4		
Heading	War Diary of 16th (Service) Battalion the Highland Light Infantry from 1st February 1916 to 29th February 1916 Volume IV		
Miscellaneous			
War Diary	F2 Sector	01/02/1916	04/02/1916
War Diary	Bouzincourt	05/02/1916	11/02/1916
War Diary	F2 Sector	12/02/1916	17/02/1916
War Diary	Millencourt	18/02/1916	24/02/1916
War Diary	Henencourt Wood	25/02/1916	29/02/1916
Miscellaneous	16th (Service) Bn H.L.I. Appendix 1	01/02/1916	01/02/1916
Miscellaneous	16th (Service) Bn H.L.I. Appendix II		
Heading	War Diary of the 16th (Service) Bn Highland Light Infantry 1st to 31st March 1916 Vol 5		
War Diary	Albert	01/03/1916	09/03/1916
War Diary	E2 Sector	10/03/1916	17/03/1916
War Diary	Dernancourt	18/03/1916	23/03/1916
War Diary	E2 Sector	24/03/1916	29/03/1916

War Diary	Albert	30/03/1916	31/03/1916
Miscellaneous	16th (Service) Battalion H.L.I. Appendix No. 1. Extract from 32nd Divisional Intelligence Summary		
Heading	97th Brigade. 32nd Division. 16th Battalion Highland Light Infantry April 1916		
Miscellaneous	To: D.A.G., General Headquarters, 3rd Echelon.	03/05/1916	03/05/1916
Heading	16th (Service) Bn H.L.I. War Diary of the 16th (Service) Bn Highland Light Infantry From 1st April, 1916 till 30th April, 1916		
War Diary	Albert	01/04/1916	04/04/1916
War Diary	Bouzincourt	04/04/1916	16/04/1916
War Diary	Authville	17/04/1916	25/04/1916
War Diary	Warloy	26/04/1916	30/04/1916
Heading	97th Brigade. 32nd Division. 16th Battalion Highland Light Infantry May 1916		
Miscellaneous	To: D.A.G., General Headquarters, 3rd Echelon.	03/06/1916	03/06/1916
Heading	War Diary of the 16th (Service) Battalion the Highland Light Infantry from to 1st May to 31st May 1916 Vol 6		
War Diary	Warloy	01/05/1916	04/05/1916
War Diary	Pierregot	05/05/1916	17/05/1916
War Diary	Senlis	18/05/1916	27/05/1916
War Diary	Blackhorse Bridge	28/05/1916	31/05/1916
Heading	97th Brigade. 32nd Division. 1/16th Battalion Highland Light Infantry June 1916		
Miscellaneous	To D.A.G. General Headquarters, 3rd Echelon	01/07/1916	01/07/1916
War Diary	Aveluy Wood	01/06/1916	07/06/1916
War Diary	Martinsart Wood	08/06/1916	10/06/1916
War Diary	Senlis	10/06/1916	12/06/1916
War Diary	Contay Wood	13/06/1916	22/06/1916
War Diary	Senlis	22/06/1916	27/06/1916
War Diary	Martmsart Wood	28/06/1916	28/06/1916
War Diary	Bouzincourt	29/06/1916	31/07/1916
Heading	Appendices 1, 2 & 3		
Miscellaneous	16th (Service) Battalion H.L.I. List Of Officers Who Went Into Action With The Battalion On 1st July, 1916	31/07/1916	31/07/1916
Miscellaneous	Appendix "A"		
Miscellaneous	Hostile Artillery Opposite 32nd Division Front.		
Miscellaneous	Particulars Of Roads Behind The German Lines.		
Miscellaneous	Thiepval		
Map	Rough Plan of The Farm Du Mouquet		
Miscellaneous	Ferme De Mouquet.		
Miscellaneous	97th Infantry Brigade Programme of Moves		
Miscellaneous	Allocation Of Trenches To Battalion Appendix H.1.		
Miscellaneous	Programme Of Preliminary Bombardment. Appendix B. 1.		
Miscellaneous	Table of Lifts for 16 pdr Batteries Appendix B. 2		
Operation(al) Order(s)	16th (Service) Battalion H.L.I. Operation Order No. 1. Appendix Z	23/06/1916	23/06/1916
Miscellaneous	16th (Service) Battalion H.L.I. List Of Casualties In Officers On 1st July, 1916.	01/07/1916	01/07/1916
Map			
Heading	War Diary of the 16th (Service) Battalion Highland Light Infantry Volume. 9. From 1st till 31st August, 1916 Vol 9		
War Diary	Bethune	01/08/1916	05/08/1916
War Diary	Cambrin Sector Left Sub-Sector	06/08/1916	06/08/1916

War Diary	Left Sub-Sector	06/08/1916	10/08/1916
War Diary	Village Line Cambrin Sector	11/08/1916	14/08/1916
War Diary	Cambrin Left Sub-Sector	15/08/1916	17/08/1916
War Diary	Annequin North	18/08/1916	21/08/1916
War Diary	Annezin	22/08/1916	23/08/1916
War Diary	Mazingarbe	24/08/1916	24/08/1916
War Diary	Hulluch Right Sub-Sector	25/08/1916	28/08/1916
War Diary	Tenth Avenue Hulluch Section	29/08/1916	31/08/1916
Heading	97th Brigade. 32nd Division. 16th Battalion Highland Light Infantry September 1916		
Miscellaneous	To: D.A.G., General Headquarters, 3rd Echelon		
Heading	War Diary of the 16th (Service) Battalion the Highland Light Infantry Volume 11 from 1st-30th September. 1916		
War Diary	Beuvry	01/09/1916	08/09/1916
War Diary	Beuvry	08/09/1916	08/09/1916
War Diary	Cuinchy Section.	09/09/1916	12/09/1916
War Diary	Le Quesnoy	13/09/1916	16/09/1916
War Diary	Cuinchy Section.	17/09/1916	26/09/1916
War Diary	Bethune	27/09/1916	30/09/1916
Heading	97th Brigade. 32nd Division. 16th Battalion Highland Light Infantry October 1916		
Miscellaneous	To: D.A.G. Base.	31/10/1916	31/10/1916
Heading	War Diary of the 16th (Service) Battalion the Highland Light Infantry Volume XI 1/31st October, 1916		
War Diary	Bethune	01/10/1916	04/10/1916
War Diary	Annequin	05/10/1916	08/10/1916
War Diary	Cambrin Section.	09/10/1916	14/10/1916
War Diary	Bethune	15/10/1916	15/10/1916
War Diary	Marles Mines.	16/10/1916	16/10/1916
War Diary	Ostreville	17/10/1916	17/10/1916
War Diary	Houvin Houvigneul	18/10/1916	18/10/1916
War Diary	Longeuvillette	19/10/1916	20/10/1916
War Diary	Rubempre.	21/10/1916	22/10/1916
War Diary	Bouzincourt	23/10/1916	29/10/1916
War Diary	Rubempre.	30/10/1916	30/10/1916
War Diary	Val De Maison	31/10/1916	31/10/1916
Heading	War Diary of the 16th (Service) Battalion High. L.I. Volume 13 from 1st to 30th November 1916 Vol 12		
War Diary	Val-De-Maison	01/11/1916	13/11/1916
War Diary	Harponville	14/11/1916	14/11/1916
War Diary	Pioneer Road	15/11/1916	15/11/1916
War Diary	Englebelmer	16/11/1916	19/11/1916
War Diary	Mailly-Maillet	20/11/1916	23/11/1916
War Diary	Raincheval	24/11/1916	25/11/1916
War Diary	Gezaincourt	26/11/1916	26/11/1916
War Diary	St Leger-L-Domart	27/11/1916	30/11/1916
Heading	97th Brigade. 32nd Division. 16th Battalion Highland Light Infantry December 1916		
War Diary	War Diary of the 16th (Service) Battalion The Highland Light Infantry Volume 1st to 31st December, 1916 Vol 13		
War Diary	St Leger-Les-Domart	01/12/1916	05/12/1916
War Diary	Lanches, Barlette, Houdaincourt	06/12/1916	16/12/1916
War Diary	Berteaucourt	17/12/1916	19/12/1916
War Diary	Rubempre	20/12/1916	31/12/1916

Heading	War Diary of the 16th (Service) Battalion High L.I. Volume 15 1st to 31st January, 1917		
War Diary	Rubempre	01/01/1917	06/01/1917
War Diary	Courcelles	07/01/1917	07/01/1917
War Diary	Serre Left Sub-Sector	08/01/1917	10/01/1917
War Diary	Courcelles	11/01/1917	12/01/1917
War Diary	Serre Left Sub-Sector	13/01/1917	14/01/1917
War Diary	Bus	15/01/1917	20/01/1917
War Diary	Beaumont Hamel	21/01/1917	23/01/1917
War Diary	R.2. Sub-Sector	24/01/1917	25/01/1917
War Diary	Beaumont Hamel	26/01/1917	27/01/1917
War Diary	R.1. Sub-Sector	28/01/1917	31/01/1917
Miscellaneous	To: Headquarters, 97th Inf Bde.	28/02/1917	28/02/1917
Heading	War Diary of the 16th (Service) Bn Highland Light Infantry Volume 16 From 1st to 28th February 1917		
War Diary	Beaumont Hamel.	01/02/1917	02/02/1917
War Diary	R.2. Subsector	03/02/1917	07/02/1917
War Diary	Beaumont Hamel	08/02/1917	12/02/1917
War Diary	R.1. Subsector	13/02/1917	14/02/1917
War Diary	Oldham Camp	15/02/1917	17/02/1917
War Diary	Pierregot	18/02/1917	21/02/1917
War Diary	Rivery	22/02/1917	22/02/1917
War Diary	Marcelcave	23/02/1917	25/02/1917
War Diary	Mezieres.	26/02/1917	27/02/1917
War Diary	Beaufort	28/02/1917	28/02/1917
Miscellaneous	To : Headquarters, 97th Infantry Brigade.	31/03/1917	31/03/1917
Miscellaneous	To : D.A.G., General Headquarters, 3rd Echelon.	31/03/1917	31/03/1917
Heading	War Diary of The 16th (Service) Battalion Highland Light Infantry Volume 17 1st to 31st March, 1917.		
War Diary	Beaufort	01/03/1917	02/03/1917
War Diary	Left Sub-Sector	03/03/1917	05/03/1917
War Diary	Warvillers	06/03/1917	08/03/1917
War Diary	Left Sub-Sector	09/03/1917	10/03/1917
War Diary	Warvillers	11/03/1917	14/03/1917
War Diary	Frwsnoy En Chaussee	15/03/1917	17/03/1917
War Diary	Le Quesnoy	18/03/1917	18/03/1917
War Diary	Fresnoy-Les Roye	18/03/1917	18/03/1917
War Diary	Nesle	20/03/1917	27/03/1917
War Diary	Ferme De Montizelle	28/03/1917	28/03/1917
War Diary	Vaux Etreillers Ch De Pommery	29/03/1917	31/03/1917
Miscellaneous	16th (Service) Bn High L.I. Honours and Awards		
Miscellaneous	To: Headquarters, 97th Inf. Bde	30/04/1917	30/04/1917
War Diary	Etreillers	01/04/1917	01/04/1917
War Diary	Vaux	02/04/1917	02/04/1917
War Diary	Roupy	03/04/1917	05/04/1917
War Diary	Attilly	06/04/1917	14/04/1917
War Diary	Gricourt St Quentin Road	15/04/1917	15/04/1917
War Diary	Germaine	16/04/1917	19/04/1917
War Diary	Offoy	20/04/1917	29/04/1917
Operation(al) Order(s)	16th (Service) Battalion H.L.I. Operation Order.	11/04/1917	11/04/1917
Miscellaneous		13/04/1917	13/04/1917
Heading	War Diary of the 16th Battalion Highland Light Infantry Volume 19 From 1st to 31st May. 1917		
War Diary	Offoy	01/05/1917	15/05/1917
War Diary	Etalon	16/05/1917	16/05/1917
War Diary	Rosieres	17/05/1917	17/05/1917

War Diary	Thennes	18/05/1917	30/05/1917
War Diary	Cachy	31/05/1917	31/05/1917
Miscellaneous	32nd Division. Appendix II.	22/05/1917	22/05/1917
Heading	War Diary of the 16th (Service) Battalion The Highland Light Infantry Volume XX From 1st to 30th June, 1917		
War Diary	Cachy	01/06/1917	01/06/1917
War Diary	Doulieu	02/06/1917	14/06/1917
War Diary	Eecke	15/06/1917	16/06/1917
War Diary	Petit Synthe	17/06/1917	18/06/1917
War Diary	Camp Juniac	19/06/1917	25/06/1917
War Diary	Nieuport	26/06/1917	29/06/1917
War Diary	Right Sub-Sector	30/06/1917	30/06/1917
War Diary	War Diary of the 16th (Service) Bn Highland Light Infantry Volume 21 1st to 31st July 1917		
War Diary	Lombardzyde	01/07/1916	04/07/1916
War Diary	Nieuport	05/07/1917	08/07/1917
War Diary	Lombardzyde	09/07/1917	12/07/1917
War Diary	Jean Bart Camp.	13/07/1917	16/07/1917
War Diary	Ghyvelde	17/07/1917	25/07/1917
War Diary	Camp D.8.a.	26/07/1917	27/07/1917
War Diary	Kuhn Camp	28/07/1917	31/07/1917
Miscellaneous	Report on the Operation of 16th Battalion The Highland Light Infantry in the Nieuport Area, "C" Sector, Right Sub-Sector, 8/11th July, 1917	08/07/1917	08/07/1917
Miscellaneous	Appendix 4		
Miscellaneous	Appendix 5	27/07/1917	27/07/1917
Miscellaneous	Appendix 6	15/07/1917	15/07/1917
Miscellaneous	Ref. 16/97.		
Miscellaneous	2 (iv) Dress	03/07/1917	03/07/1917
Miscellaneous	To : Headquarters, 97th Infantry Brigade. Report on "B" Raid on point M.23.a.1.3 by 16th Battalion The Highland Light Infantry, on night of 4/5th July, 1917	06/07/1917	06/07/1917
Heading	War Diary of the 16th Battalion The Highland Light Infantry Volume XXII From 1st to 31st August, 1917		
War Diary	Khun Camp	01/08/1917	10/08/1917
War Diary	Jeanniot Camp	11/08/1917	15/08/1917
War Diary	Bray Dunes	16/08/1917	18/08/1917
War Diary	Ghyvelde	20/08/1917	27/08/1917
War Diary	Jeanniot Camp.	28/08/1917	28/08/1917
War Diary	Khun Camp.	29/08/1917	31/08/1917
Heading	War Diary of the 16th Battalion Highland Light Infantry Volume XXIII from 1st to 30th September 1917		
War Diary	Khun Camp	01/09/1917	03/09/1917
War Diary	St. Georges Sector	04/09/1917	09/09/1917
War Diary	Oost Dunkerke	10/09/1917	15/09/1917
War Diary	St Georges Sector	16/09/1917	20/09/1917
War Diary	Khun Camp	21/09/1917	21/09/1917
War Diary	La Panne	22/09/1917	22/09/1917
War Diary	Fort De Dunes	23/09/1917	24/09/1917
War Diary	La Panne	25/09/1917	28/09/1917
War Diary	Nieuport	29/09/1917	30/09/1917
Heading	War Diary of the 16th Bn Highland Light Infantry Volume XXIV from 1st to 31st October, 1917		
War Diary	Nieuport	01/10/1917	02/10/1917
War Diary	Lombardzyde Right Subsector	03/10/1917	05/10/1917
War Diary	Coxyde	06/10/1917	06/10/1917

War Diary	Teteghem	07/10/1917	24/10/1917
War Diary	Eringhem	25/10/1917	25/10/1917
War Diary	Broxeele	26/10/1917	31/10/1917
Heading	War Diary of the 16th Battalion Highland Light Infantry Volume XXV 1st till 30th Nov. 1917		
War Diary	Broxeele	01/11/1917	10/11/1917
War Diary	Camp at J.7.a.3.3	11/11/1917	11/11/1917
War Diary	Road Camp	12/11/1917	22/11/1917
War Diary	Irish Farm	23/11/1917	23/11/1917
War Diary	Wurst Farm	24/11/1917	25/11/1917
War Diary	Passchendaele Sector	25/11/1917	27/11/1917
War Diary	Farm Wurst Camp	28/11/1917	28/11/1917
War Diary	Irish Farm	29/11/1917	30/11/1917
Heading	War Diary of the 16th Highland Light Infantry Volume XXVI 1st to 31st December 1917		
Map	Note: Areas Shewn Wet Not Necessarily Impassable		
War Diary	Bellvue	01/12/1917	01/12/1917
War Diary	Battle Position	01/12/1917	04/12/1917
War Diary	Brake Camp	05/12/1917	07/12/1917
War Diary	Irish Farm	08/12/1917	17/12/1917
War Diary	Hilltop Farm	18/12/1917	20/12/1917
War Diary	Left Subsector	21/12/1917	23/12/1917
War Diary	Siege Camp	24/12/1917	30/12/1917
War Diary	Louches	31/12/1917	31/12/1917
Miscellaneous	List of officers who went into action with the Battalion on 1/2nd December. 1917.	01/12/1917	01/12/1917
Miscellaneous	To : Officers Commanding All Companies.	01/12/1917	01/12/1917
Miscellaneous	16th Highland Light Infantry (No. 2. Battalion) Operation Orders	29/11/1917	29/11/1917
Miscellaneous	Notes To Accompany Operation Orders.	28/11/1917	28/11/1917
Miscellaneous	16th Highland Light Infantry Amendment To Operation Order	30/11/1917	30/11/1917
Heading	War Diary of the 16th Battalion the Highland Light Infantry Volume XXVII from 1st to 31st January 1918		
War Diary	Louches	01/01/1918	20/01/1918
War Diary	P Camp	21/01/1918	25/01/1918
War Diary	B.3.C.2.6.	26/01/1918	26/01/1918
War Diary	Het Sas	27/01/1918	31/01/1918
War Diary	To "A" Headquarters, 32nd Division.	28/02/1917	28/02/1917
War Diary	To : D.A.G., General Headquarters, 3rd Echelon.	28/02/1917	28/02/1917
Heading	War Diary of the 16th Battalion Regiment Light Infantry Volume XXVIII from 1st to 28th February 1918		
War Diary	Het Sas	01/02/1918	01/02/1918
War Diary	Baboon Camp	02/02/1918	04/02/1918
War Diary	Het Sas	05/02/1918	19/02/1918
War Diary	Baboon Camp	20/02/1918	26/02/1918
War Diary	Boesighne Camp	27/02/1918	28/02/1918
Miscellaneous	To: D.A.G., General Headquarters 3rd Echelon	30/04/1918	30/04/1918
Heading	War Diary of the 16th Battalion The Highland Light Infantry Volume 18 from 1st to 30th April 1917		
War Diary	Offoy	30/04/1918	30/04/1918
Miscellaneous	16th (Service) Battalion H.L.I. Congratulatory Messages received for Operation of 14th April, 1917. Appendix I	14/04/1917	14/04/1917
Miscellaneous	16th (Service) Battalion H.L.I. Preliminary Operation Order. Appendix 2		

WO 95/24075
A1 INF @ DC
16 SIN HLI

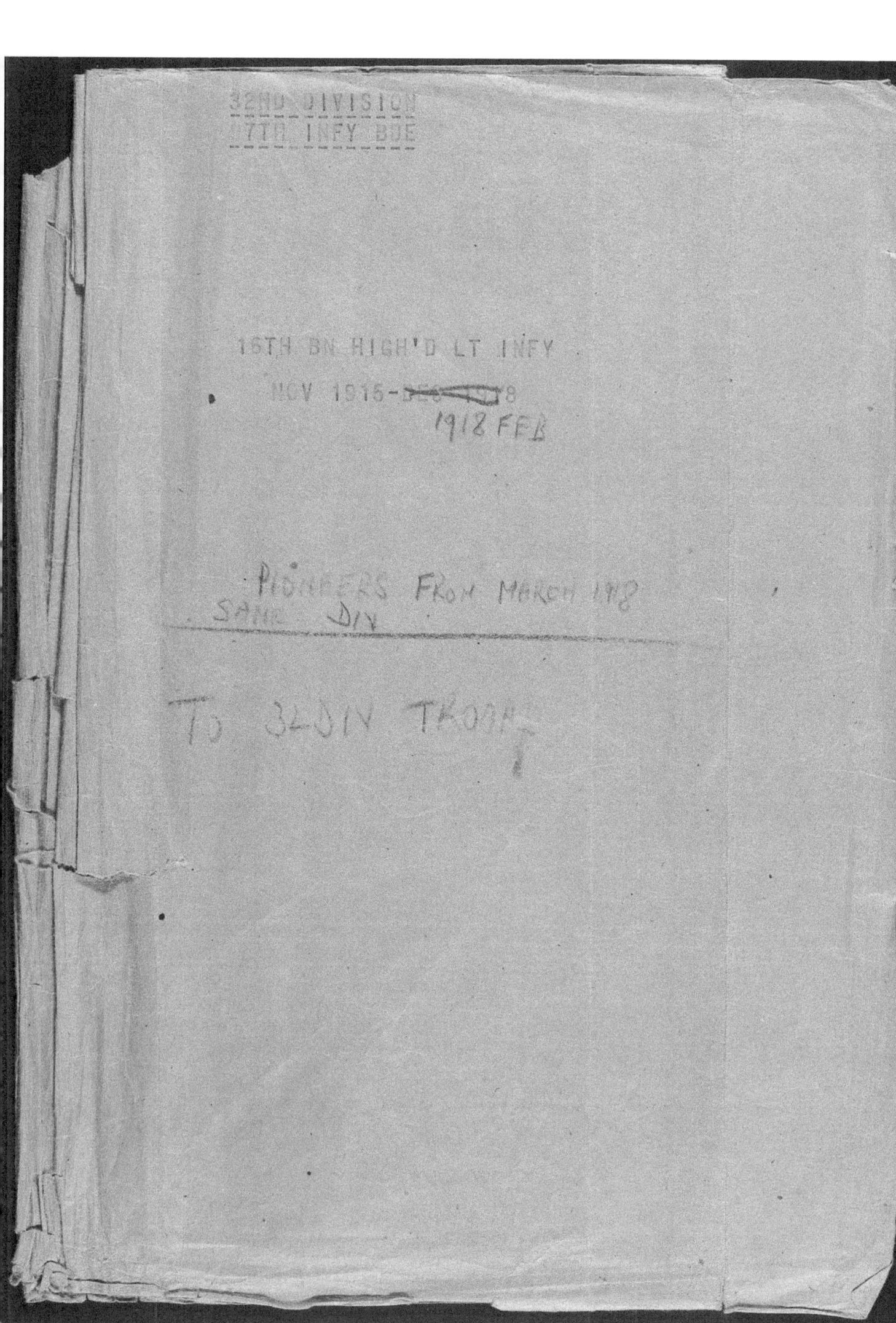

32ND DIVISION
97TH INFY BDE

16TH BN HIGH'D LT INFY
NOV 1915 – 1918
1918 FEB

PIONEERS FROM MARCH 1918
SAME DIV

TO 34DIV TROOPS

Confidential

War Diary

of

16th (Service) Battalion The Highland Light Infantry

From 23rd November, 1915   To 31st December, 1915

Volume II

Army Form C. 2118.

WAR DIARY
or
INTELLIGENCE SUMMARY.

(Erase heading not required.)

Instructions regarding War Diaries and Intelligence Summaries are contained in F. S. Regs., Part II. and the Staff Manual respectively. Title pages will be prepared in manuscript.

Place	Date	Hour	Summary of Events and Information	Remarks and references to Appendices

*353 Wt. W2544/1454 700,000 5/15 D. D. & L. A.D.S.S./Forms/C. 2118.

97/32

North r/Bec. 1915

16th MZ.?
, folo 1, 2, 3

32nd

I.P.
9 sheets

Volume B Page 1

WAR DIARY
or
INTELLIGENCE SUMMARY.
(Erase heading not required.)

Army Form C. 2118.

Instructions regarding War Diaries and Intelligence Summaries are contained in F. S. Regs., Part II. and the Staff Manual respectively. Title pages will be prepared in manuscript.

Place	Date	Hour	Summary of Events and Information	Remarks and references to Appendices
CODFORD	23/11/15	7am	The Battalion left CODFORD in two trains for FOLKESTONE where they embarked for BOULOGNE. Total Strength 30 Officers 1008 Other Ranks, this includes advance Party which proceeded via SOUTHAMPTON and HAVRE	List of Officers Appendix I
BOULOGNE	23/11/15	4pm	The Battalion arrived at BOULOGNE and proceeded to the REST CAMP	w/t
— do —	24/11/15		The Battalion remained in Camp all day and then paraded at 11.30pm for entrainment at CENTRAL STATION BOULOGNE	w/t
— do —	25/11/15	12.20am	The Battalion entrained and proceeded to LONGPRE arriving there at 4am where detrainment took place	w/t
LONGPRE	25/11/15	5.30am	The Battalion proceeded to SURCAMPS and VAUCHELLES where they were accommodated in Billets. The Advance Party joined the Battalion at this point.	w/t
SURCAMPS and VAUCHELLES	26/11/15		The Battalion remained in Billets :- CASUALTY one Other Ranks accidentally wounded	w/t
— do —	27/11/15	8.50am	The Battalion paraded and proceeded to ST VAST EN CHAUSSEE arriving there at 1pm and were Billetted there for the night	w/t
ST VAST EN CHAUSSEE	28/11/15	8am	The Battalion proceeded to PIERREGOT arriving there at 2pm and went into Billets	w/t

Volume II Page 2

Army Form C. 2118.

WAR DIARY
or
INTELLIGENCE SUMMARY.
(Erase heading not required.)

Place	Date	Hour	Summary of Events and Information	Remarks and references to Appendices
PIERREGOT	29/11/15		In Billets at PIERREGOT	wsl
— do —	30/11/15		— do — — do —	wsl
— do —	1/12/15		The Battalion is attached to the 51st Division from this date for training in Trench Warfare and paraded at 9 am to proceed to SENLIS and MARTINSART; Headquarters (less Machine Gun Section) A & B Coys to SENLIS, C & D Coys and Machine Gun Section to MARTINSART arriving there at 12.30pm & 1.3.30pm respectively reporting to Headquarters 152nd Infantry Brigade. Officers & N.C.Os in Trenches 24 hours — Platoon 24 hours — Companies 24 hours — Battalion 72 hours —	
SENLIS and MARTINSART	2/12/15		Officers & Non Commissioned Officers & C & D Companies were attached to the 6th Seaforth Highlanders & 6 & 8th R Argylls for training in G1, G2, G3, Sectors (North & East of MARTINSART VILLAGE THIEPVAL WOOD) The Battalion remaining in Billets in SENLIS and under canvas at MARTINSART	wsl
— do —	3/12/15		Officers & Non Commissioned Officers of A & B Companies were attached to 6R Seaforth Highlanders & 6 & 8th R Argylls for training	wsl
— do —	4/12/15		Platoons in C and D Companies were attached to the 6R Seaforth & 6 R Argylls for training	wsl
— do —	5/12/15		Platoons A & B. Companies were attached to 6R Seaforth & 8R Argylls for training	wsl

Volume 2 Page 3

Army Form C. 2118.

WAR DIARY
or
INTELLIGENCE SUMMARY.

(Erase heading not required.)

Instructions regarding War Diaries and Intelligence Summaries are contained in F. S. Regs., Part II. and the Staff Manual respectively. Title pages will be prepared in manuscript.

Place	Date	Hour	Summary of Events and Information	Remarks and references to Appendices
SENLIS and MARTINSART	6/9/15		C & D Companies were attached to 8th Argylls and 6th Seaforths	wst
	8/9/15		A & B Companies attached to 6th Seaforths & 8th Argylls. Casualties one Other Ranks wounded	wst
Note G3	9/9/15		The Battalion relieved the 6th Seaforths in G3 Sector (North and East sides of AVELUY WOOD) Relief completed by 4 pm. Owing to the very inadequate dug-out accommodation it was necessary to send two platoons into Reserve at MARTINSART. The Battalion settled down wonderfully and the critical question of feeding was got over.	wst
— do —	10/9/15		The Battalion suffered their first loss. Pte J014931 N Kitchen A Company killed in Action	wst
— do —	11/9/15		The Battalion was relieved by the 5th Gordons in G3 Sector at 4.30 pm and proceeded to SENLIS and MARTINSART	wst
SENLIS and MARTINSART	12/9/15		The Battalion moved from SENLIS and MARTINSART into Billets at PIERREGOT arriving there at 2.30 pm	wst
PIERREGOT	13/9/15		In Billets at PIERREGOT carrying out instruction in Grenade Throwing etc.	wst
— do —	14/9/15		In Billets at PIERREGOT carrying out instruction in Grenade Throwing etc.	wst

Army Form C. 2118.

Volume 2 page 4

WAR DIARY
or
INTELLIGENCE SUMMARY.

(Erase heading not required.)

Instructions regarding War Diaries and Intelligence Summaries are contained in F. S. Regs., Part II. and the Staff Manual respectively. Title pages will be prepared in manuscript.

Place	Date	Hour	Summary of Events and Information	Remarks and references to Appendices
PIERREGOT	15/12/15		In Billets at PIERREGOT	
— do —	16/12/15		Carrying out Instruction	
— do —	17/12/15		in Grenade throwing	
— do —	18/12/15		etc.	
— do —	19/12/15			
— do —	20/12/15			
— do —	21/12/15			
— do —	22/12/15		The Battalion moved from PIERREGOT and went into Billets at MARTINSART.	
MARTINSART	23/12/15		The Battalion relieved the 6th Seaforths in F2 Sector (North East corner of AUTHUILLE WOOD from point X1A44 to point X7B45 Reference Map OVILLERS 57d S.E.4 2nd Edition) 17th H.L.I. on Right in F1 Sector.	
— do —	24/12/15		No. 14170 Private A Gourlay accidentally killed. In occupancy of F2 Sector.	
F2 Sector	25/12/15		In occupancy of F2 Sector	

Volume 2. Page 5

Army Form C. 2118.

WAR DIARY
or
INTELLIGENCE SUMMARY.
(Erase heading not required.)

Instructions regarding War Diaries and Intelligence Summaries are contained in F. S. Regs., Part II. and the Staff Manual respectively. Title pages will be prepared in manuscript.

Place	Date	Hour	Summary of Events and Information	Remarks and references to Appendices
Eg Sector	26/9/15		In occupancy of F.2 Sector	
— do —	27/9/15		Battalion relieved in F2 Sector by the 15th H.L.I. relief complete by 4 p.m. and Battalion proceeded into Billets at AVELUY	west
AVELUY	28/9/15		The Battalion in Brigade Support at AVELUY	west
— do —	29/9/15			
— do —	30/9/15			
— do —	31/9/15		The Battalion relieved the 15th H.L.I. in F2 Sub. Sector relief complete by 4 p.m. 17th H.L.I. on right in F.1 Sector. Strength of Battalion at this date Officers 30 Other Ranks 999	A.D.S.

16th (Service) Battalion H.L.I.

APPENDIX 1

LIST OF OFFICERS

Lt Col. & Hon. Col.,	Laidlaw D.
Major	Kyle. R.
"	McElwain
Captain & Adjutant	Scott. W.D.
Captain	Fraser G.S.
"	Reid F.W.
"	Robinson W.E.
"	Alexander J.
"	Cameron C.A.
"	Kerr D.B.
"	Hunter J.
Lieutenant	Middleton T.
"	McLaren W.
"	Blackie A.F.
"	Garrett-Fisher W.E.
"	Wilkie J.S.
"	McPherson A.
"	Caulfield G.
"	Johnston T.
2nd Lieutenant	Brown R.S.
"	Gemmill J.A.
"	Murdoch J.
"	Smith A.C.
"	Wilson A.P.
"	Stewart R.B.
"	Bogue R.A.
"	McDermid D.R.
"	Andrew H.T.
Lieut. & Qr Master	Simpson R.
Lieut (R.A.M.C.)	Badcock V.E. (Medical Officer)

Confidential

War Diary
of
16th (Service) Battalion The Highland Light Infantry

From 1st January, 1916   to 31st January, 1916

Volume III

Army Form C. 2118.

WAR DIARY
or
INTELLIGENCE SUMMARY.

(Erase heading not required.)

Instructions regarding War Diaries and Intelligence Summaries are contained in F. S. Regs., Part II. and the Staff Manual respectively. Title pages will be prepared in manuscript.

Place	Date	Hour	Summary of Events and Information	Remarks and references to Appendices

#353 Wt. W2544/1454 700,000 5/15 D. D. & L. A.D.S.S./Forms/C. 2118.

Army Form C. 2118.

Volume IV Page 1

Instructions regarding War Diaries and Intelligence
Summaries are contained in F. S. Regs., Part II.
and the Staff Manual respectively. Title pages
will be prepared in manuscript.

WAR DIARY
or
INTELLIGENCE SUMMARY.
(Erase heading not required.)

Place	Date	Hour	Summary of Events and Information	Remarks and references to Appendices
32 Sector	1/1/16		In occupancy of 32 Sector. The 17th Y.L.I. on our right in 31 Sector. Casualties one other Rank wounded	nil
	2/1/16		In occupancy of 32 Sector	nil
	3/1/16		In occupancy of 32 Sector. Casualties 2 other Ranks wounded	nil
	4/1/16		In occupancy of 32 Sector. Casualties 1 Other Rank killed in Action 1 other Ranks wounded	nil
	5/1/16		In occupancy of 32 Sector	nil
	6/1/16		In occupancy of 33 Sector. One other Rank killed in Action Lieut J.A. Gemmell wounded 2 Other Ranks wounded	nil
	7/1/16		The Battalion relieved in 32 Sector by the 2nd K.O.Y.L.I. relief complete by 11.30pm The Battalion men less "D" Company went into Billets at BOUZINCOURT "D" Company into Billets at AVELUY	nil
BOUZINCOURT and AVELUY	9/1/16 to 13/1/16		Battalion in Billets at BOUZINCOURT and AVELUY. Lieutenant Gemmell reported for duty 12-1-16	nil

#353 Wt. W2544/1454 700,000 5/15 D. D. & L. A.D.S.S./Forms/C. 2118.

Volume III Page 2.

Army Form C. 2118.

WAR DIARY
or
INTELLIGENCE SUMMARY.
(Erase heading not required.)

Instructions regarding War Diaries and Intelligence Summaries are contained in F. S. Regs., Part II. and the Staff Manual respectively. Title pages will be prepared in manuscript.

Place	Date	Hour	Summary of Events and Information	Remarks and references to Appendices
BOUZINCOURT and AVELUY	14/1/16		The Battalion relieved the 2nd K.O.Y.L.I. in F2 sector relief complete at 4.30pm. The 17th H.L.I. on our right in F1 sector	WD
F2 sector	15/1/16		In occupancy of F2 sector. Casualties Nil	WD
	16/1/16		In occupancy of F2 sector. Casualties Nil	WD
	17/1/16		In occupancy of F2 sector. Casualties Nil	WD
	18/1/16		In occupancy of F2 sector. Casualties Nil	WD
	19/1/16		In occupancy of F2 sector. Casualties One Other Ranks wounded	WD
	20/1/16		In occupancy of F2 sector. Casualties One Other Ranks killed in Action	WD
	21/1/16		Battalion relieved by the 2nd K.O.Y.L.I. and proceeded into Billets at AVELUY. Casualties one Other Ranks killed in Action	WD
	22/1/16 to 29/1/16		In Billets at AVELUY	WD

Volume 3 Page 3

Army Form C. 2118.

WAR DIARY
or
INTELLIGENCE SUMMARY.

(Erase heading not required.)

Instructions regarding War Diaries and Intelligence Summaries are contained in F.S. Regs., Part II. and the Staff Manual respectively. Title pages will be prepared in manuscript.

Place	Date	Hour	Summary of Events and Information	Remarks and references to Appendices
AVELUY	28/1/16		The Battalion relieved the 2nd K.O.Y.L.I. and 3a Sector. Relief complete by 12 Noon. Battalion on right 17th H.L.I. 2nd Manchester Regt. on left.	w.o.s
3a Sector	29/1/16		In occupancy of 3/2 Sector. Casualties One Other Ranks killed in action, One Other Ranks wounded. Battalion	w.o.s
	30/1/16		In occupancy of 3/2 Sector. Casualties 3 Other Ranks Wounded	w.o.s
	31/1/16		In occupancy of 3/2 Sector. Casualties 1 Other Ranks Killed in Action	w.o.s
			Strength of Battalion Officers 30 Other Ranks 950	

32

16th H.L.I.

Vol. A

G.P.

Confidential

War Diary

of

16th (Service) Battalion The Highland Light Infantry

From 1st February, 1916   To 29th February, 1916

Volume IV

Army Form C. 2118.

WAR DIARY
or
INTELLIGENCE SUMMARY.
(Erase heading not required.)

Instructions regarding War Diaries and Intelligence Summaries are contained in F. S. Regs., Part II. and the Staff Manual respectively. Title pages will be prepared in manuscript.

Place	Date	Hour	Summary of Events and Information	Remarks and references to Appendices

#353 Wt. W2544/1454 700,000 5/15 D. D. & L. A.D.S.S./Forms/C. 2118.

Volume II Page 1

Army Form C. 2118.

WAR DIARY
or
INTELLIGENCE SUMMARY.
(Erase heading not required.)

Instructions regarding War Diaries and Intelligence Summaries are contained in F. S. Regs., Part II. and the Staff Manual respectively. Title pages will be prepared in manuscript.

Place	Date	Hour	Summary of Events and Information	Remarks and references to Appendices
F.2 Sector	1/3/16		In occupancy of F.2 Sector 17th K.L.I. on our right 2nd Manchesters on our left. Other Ranks Wounded one Other Ranks Wounded 1 Missing one	See Appendix No 1
	2/3/16		In occupancy of F.2 Sector	wdi
	3/3/16		In occupancy of F.2 Sector 2nd Lieut. J.S. Hodgkinson taken on Strength of Unit	wdi
	4/3/16		Relieved by 2nd K.O.Y.L.I. Relief complete by 2 pm Battalion proceeded to Billets at BOUZINCOURT.	wdi
BOUZINCOURT	5/3/16		In Billets at BOUZINCOURT	wdi
	6/3/16		do	wdi
	7/3/16		do	wdi
	8/3/16		do	wdi
	9/3/16		do 16th K.L.I. called up to support 2nd K.O.Y.L.I. in F.2 Sector	See Appendix No 2
	10/3/16		do 2 Platoons in F.2 Sector	wdi
	11/3/16		Other Ranks wounded one Relieved 2nd Bn K.O.Y.L.I. in F.2 Sector Relief complete by 12.30pm	wdi
F.2 Sector	12/3/16		In occupancy of F.2 Sector Other Ranks wounded 2 2nd Bn Inniskilling Fusiliers on our left 17th K.L.I. on our right	wdi

#353 Wt. W2544/1454 700,000 5/15 D. D. & L. A.D.S.S./Forms/C. 2118.

Volume II Page 8

Army Form C. 2118.

WAR DIARY
or
INTELLIGENCE SUMMARY.
(Erase heading not required.)

Instructions regarding War Diaries and Intelligence Summaries are contained in F. S. Regs., Part II. and the Staff Manual respectively. Title pages will be prepared in manuscript.

Place	Date	Hour	Summary of Events and Information	Remarks and references to Appendices
32 Sector	13/3/16		In occupancy of 32 Sector 5th K.O.Y.L.I. on our left 17th H.L.I., on our right. Other ranks wounded 4	Seen
	14/3/16		In occupancy of 32 Sector 5th K.O.Y.L.I. on our left 17th H.L.I., on our right. Other ranks wounded 2	Seen
	15/3/16		In occupancy of 32 Sector 5th K.O.Y.L.I. on our left 17th H.L.I., on our right. Other ranks killed in Action 2	Seen
	16/3/16		In occupancy of 32 Sector. K.O.Y.L.I. on our left. 17th H.L.I., on our right. 2nd Lieutenants J. Cooper and J.A. Brown taken to strength of Unit.	Seen
	17/3/16		Relieved by 16th Northumberland Fusiliers. Relief complete at 12.30pm	Seen
MILLENCOURT	18/3/16		In Billets at MILLENCOURT. Lieut. W.E. Gauntt Fisher struck off Strength. Evacuated to U.K. sick	Seen
	19/3/16		do	Seen
	20/3/16		do	Seen
	21/3/16		do	Seen
	22/3/16		do	Seen
	23/3/16		do	Seen
	24/3/16		do	Seen

Volume II Page 3

Army Form C. 2118.

Instructions regarding War Diaries and Intelligence Summaries are contained in F. S. Regs., Part II. and the Staff Manual respectively. Title pages will be prepared in manuscript.

WAR DIARY
or
INTELLIGENCE SUMMARY.
(Erase heading not required.)

Place	Date	Hour	Summary of Events and Information	Remarks and references to Appendices
HENENCOURT WOOD	25/8/16		In (Bivouac) Hutments at HENENCOURT WOOD	and
	26/8/16		do do	and
	27/8/16		do do	and
	28/8/16		do do	and
	29/8/16		do do	and
	29/8/16		The Battalion moved out of HUTMENTS at HENENCOURT WOOD to Billets in ALBERT at 2pm	and
	29/8/16		In Billets at ALBERT	and

#353 Wt. W3544/1454 700,000 5/15 D. D. & L. A.D.S.S./Forms/C. 2118.

16th (Service) Bn H.L.I.

APPENDIX 1

1st February, 1916.

At 11.45p.m., what was evidently a carefully planned enterprise was carried by a bombing party of the enemy. The party bombed the two sentries occupying listening post No. 6 in trench 140.

One bomb was thrown which wounded both men, one evidently very badly, and the other slightly.

The slightly wounded sentry rushed back for assistance, meanwhile the noise OF THE BOMB

explosion was heard in the Fire trench. Machine Gun and heavy rifle fire was at once directed towards the sap end. A party of four men at once proceeded to the sap to bring in the wounded man. Just when they had started 25 whizzbangs in quick succession landed at various points along the parapet. Our parapet was simply raked, but luckily no one was hurt. Whenever the 'Straff' ceased the rescue party proceeded to the sap head, but found the wounded man missing. His cap, overcoat, and a German dagger were found in the trench. This morning a German disc bomb was found in the trench, and two parts of the missing man's leather jerkin. the missing man was evidently dragged out through th the wire, as the traces of blood denote. As the night was very dark the strength of the enemy party is not known.

W. D. Scott
Capt & Adjt
16th H.L.I.

16th (Service) Bn H.L.I.

APPENDIX 11

On 9th February 1916., while in billets at BOUZINCOURT, the Battalion, was warned to 'Stand To' at 6.30p.m., and then ordered to proceed to AVELUY.

At 8.15p.m., one Company was ordered to occupy the BRIDGE-HEAD TRENCHES, and remain in support of 2nd K.O.Y.L.I., in F2 Sector, who had been raided by the Germans after an intense artillery bombardment.

At 8.45p.m., the Battalion (less one Company) was ordered to return to BOUZINCOURT.

At midnight two platoons were called to proceed to F2 Sector and supply working parties.

At 9.30a.m., (10th) the other two platoons were ordered to rejoin the Battalion at BOUZINCOURT.

The two platoons which were attached to the 2nd K.O.Y.L.I., remained until the 2nd K.O.Y.L.I., were relieved by the 16th H.L.I., on 11th February, 1916.

Wm D. Scott
Capt & Adjt
16th H.L.I.

Confidential

XXX"
16 H.L.I
Vol $5

H.P
6 sheets

War Diary
of the
16th (Service) Bn. Highland Light Infantry

1st to 31st March, 1916.

Volume I Page 1

Army Form C. 2118.

WAR DIARY
or
INTELLIGENCE SUMMARY.
(Erase heading not required.)

Instructions regarding War Diaries and Intelligence Summaries are contained in F. S. Regs., Part II. and the Staff Manual respectively. Title pages will be prepared in manuscript.

Place	Date	Hour	Summary of Events and Information	Remarks and references to Appendices
ALBERT	1/3/16		In Billets at ALBERT	nil
	2/3/16		Do	nil
	3/3/16		Do. One Platoon of A Company in occupancy of TARA REDOUBT	nil
	4/3/16		Do Do	nil
	5/3/16		Do Do	nil
	6/3/16		Do Do	nil
	7/3/16		Do Do	nil
	8/3/16		Do Do	nil
	9/3/16		Do Do	nil
E2 SECTOR	10/3/16		16th H.L.I. relieved 2nd K.O.Y.L.I. in E2 SECTOR Relief complete by 1.30 pm Battalion on right 17th H.L.I. Battalion on left 1st Dorsets. 1 Other Ranks Killed in Action. 1 Other Ranks Wounded	nil
	11/3/16		In occupancy of E2 Sector. 1 O.R. Killed in Action. 2 Other Ranks Wounded	nil

Volume I Page 2

Army Form C. 2118.

WAR DIARY
or
INTELLIGENCE SUMMARY.

(Erase heading not required.)

Instructions regarding War Diaries and Intelligence Summaries are contained in F. S. Regs., Part II. and the Staff Manual respectively. Title pages will be prepared in manuscript.

Place	Date	Hour	Summary of Events and Information	Remarks and references to Appendices
E.2 SECTOR	12/3/16		In occupancy of E.2 SECTOR. 2nd Lieutenants J.C. Kelly and J. Laing joined	WOJ
	13/3/16		In occupancy of E.2 SECTOR. 7 Other Ranks wounded	WOJ
	14/3/16		In occupancy of E.2 SECTOR.	WOJ
	15/3/16		In occupancy of E.2 SECTOR.	WOJ
	16/3/16		In occupancy of E.2 SECTOR. Battalion on right 17th H.L.I. Battalion on left 2nd Manchesters. 1 Other Ranks wounded	WOJ
	17/3/16		Relieved by 2nd K.O.Y.L.I. Relief complete 10.30 a.m. One Other Ranks wounded	WOJ
DERNAN-COURT	18/3/16		In Billets at DERNANCOURT. "C" Company in support BECOURT WOOD	WOJ
	19/3/16		Do Do	WOJ
	20/3/16		Do Do One Other Ranks wounded	WOJ

Army Form C. 2118.

WAR DIARY
or
INTELLIGENCE SUMMARY.
(Erase heading not required.)

Volume I Page 3

Instructions regarding War Diaries and Intelligence Summaries are contained in F.S. Regs., Part II. and the Staff Manual respectively. Title pages will be prepared in manuscript.

Place	Date	Hour	Summary of Events and Information	Remarks and references to Appendices
DERNAN-COURT	21/3/16		In Billets at DERNANCOURT "C" Company in Support BECOURT WOOD	wts
	22/3/16		Do Do Do	wts
	23/3/16		One other ranks accidentally wounded	wts
			16th K.L.I relieved 2nd K.O.Y.L.I in E2 Sector Relief complete by 1.30pm	wts
			17th K.L.I on night June Doroute on 23rd	
E2 SECTOR	24/3/16		In occupancy of E2 Sector	wts
	25/3/16		Do	wts
	26/3/16		Do	wts
	27/3/16		Do 2nd Lieutenant J.C. Kelly Killed in Action	wts See Appendix No 1
			14 Other Ranks Killed in Action 24 other ranks wounded	
	28/3/16		In occupancy of E2 SECTOR 17th K.L. I on night 2nd Manchester on left	wts
	29/3/16		Relieved by 2nd K.O.Y.L.I Relief complete by 11.30pm 11.30 am	wts

Army Form C. 2118.

Volume V Page 4

WAR DIARY
or
INTELLIGENCE SUMMARY.

(Erase heading not required.)

Instructions regarding War Diaries and Intelligence Summaries are contained in F. S. Regs., Part II. and the Staff Manual respectively. Title pages will be prepared in manuscript.

Place	Date	Hour	Summary of Events and Information	Remarks and references to Appendices
ALBERT	30/3/16		In Billets at ALBERT. one Platoon "D" Company in TARA REDOUBT	
	31/3/16		Do. Do. Do.	

16th (Service) Battalion H.L.I.

Appendix No. 1.

Extract from 32nd Divisional Intelligence Summary

The 16th H.L.I. who were manning the parapet of trenches X20.2 to X20.4 and covering the operations of the 1st Dorset raiding party with rifle and Machine Gun fire suffered somewhat heavy casualties from hostile artillery.

97th Brigade.

32nd Division.

16th BATTALION

HIGHLAND LIGHT INFANTRY

APRIL 1916

To : D.A.G.,
   General Headquarters,
      3rd ECHELON.

   WAR DIARY of the 16th (Service) Bn Highland Light Infantry for the month of April, herewith.

               A.P. Wilson
                  2nd Lieutenant,
                  and Acting Adjutant,
                  16th (Service) Battalion H.L.I.

3rd May, 1916.

Confidential

16th (Service) Bn. H.L.I.

War Diary

of the

16th (Service) Bn. Highland Light Infantry

From 1st April, 1916 till 30th April, 1916

WAR DIARY or INTELLIGENCE SUMMARY

Army Form C. 2118

Volume 6 Page 1

Instructions regarding War Diaries and Intelligence Summaries are contained in F.S. Regs., Part II. and the Staff Manual respectively. Title Pages will be prepared in manuscript.

(Erase heading not required.)

Place	Date	Hour	Summary of Events and Information	Remarks and references to Appendices
ALBERT	1/4/16		In Billets at ALBERT. One Platoon "D" Company in TARA REDOUBT	
	2/4/16		Do. Do.	
	3/4/16		3 Other Ranks wounded.	
	4/4/16		In Billets at ALBERT. Do. Do.	
BOUZINCOURT	4/4/16	11am	In Billets at BOUZINCOURT. "A" and "B" Companies in Billets ALBERT. One O.R. Wounded in Action	
	5/4/16		In Billets at BOUZINCOURT. "A" and "C" Companies in Billets ALBERT. One Other Rank Wounded in Action	
	6/4/16		In Billets at BOUZINCOURT. Do.	
	7/4/16		Do.	

Volume 6. Page 2.

WAR DIARY
INTELLIGENCE SUMMARY

Army Form C. 2118

Place	Date	Hour	Summary of Events and Information	Remarks and references to Appendices
BOUZINCOURT	8/4/16		In Billets at BOUZINCOURT	local
	9/4/16		Do.	local
	10/4/16		Do.	local
	11/4/16		Do.	local
	12/4/16		Battalion relieved 15th H.L.I. in THIEPVAL SUBSECTOR Relief complete by 11pm Battalion on right 17th H.L.I. Battalion on left 9th Innis Fusiliers Other Ranks wounded 3	local
	13/4/16		In occupancy of THIEPVAL SUBSECTOR	local
	14/4/16		Do.	local
	15/4/16		Do. Other ranks wounded 1	local
	16/4/16		Battalion relieved by 2nd R.oy. L.I. relief complete by 10pm Battalion moved into AUTHUILLE	local

Volume 6 Page 3

WAR DIARY
or
INTELLIGENCE SUMMARY

(Erase heading not required.)

Army Form C. 2118

Place	Date	Hour	Summary of Events and Information	Remarks and references to Appendices
AUTHUILLE	17/4/16		In occupancy of AUTHUILLE	
	18/4/16		Do.	
	19/4/16		Do.	
	20/4/16		Do. 16th H.L.I. relieved 2nd R. Oyl. L.I. in THIEPVAL SUBSECTOR Relief complete by 10 pm. OR wounded 2	
	21/4/16		In occupancy of THIEPVAL SUBSECTOR Battalion on right 11th H.L.I. Battalion on left 11th Inniskilling Fusiliers	
	22/4/16		Do. Do. Other Ranks died of Wounds 2 OR Wounded 7	
	23/4/16		Do. Do. Other Ranks died of Wounds 1 OR Wounded 3	
	24/4/16		Do. 16th H.L.I. relieved by 16th Lancashire Fusiliers Relief complete by 11H.45pm Battalion moved into Billets at WARLOY	
	25/4/16		In Billets at WARLOY	

Army Form C. 2118

Volume 6 page 4.

WAR DIARY
or
INTELLIGENCE SUMMARY
(Erase heading not required.)

Instructions regarding War Diaries and Intelligence Summaries are contained in F. S. Regs., Part II. and the Staff Manual respectively. Title Pages will be prepared in manuscript.

Place	Date	Hour	Summary of Events and Information	Remarks and references to Appendices
WARLOY	26/4/16		In Billets at WARLOY	
	27/4/16		Do Do	
	28/4/16		Do Do	
	29/4/16		Do Do	
	30/4/16		Do Do	

97th Brigade.

32nd Division.

16th BATTALION

HIGHLAND LIGHT INFANTRY

MAY 1 9 1 6

To : D.A.G.,
  General Headquarters,
  3rd Echelon.

———————

  Herewith Volume 6, War Diary of
the 16th (Service) Battalion The Highland
Light Infantry.

                    W. D. Scott
                Captain & Adjutant,
            16th (Service) Battalion H.L.I.,

3rd June, 1916.

Confidential.

War Diary
of the
16th (Service) Battalion The Highland Light Infantry.
from
1st May to 31st May, 1916.

WAR DIARY
or
INTELLIGENCE SUMMARY

(Erase heading not required.)

Volume 6

Army Form C. 2118

Place	Date	Hour	Summary of Events and Information	Remarks and references to Appendices
WARLOY	1/5/16		In Billets at WARLOY-BAILLON	
	2/5/16		Do.	
	3/5/16		Do.	
	4/5/16		Do.	
PIERREGOT	5/5/16		The Battalion proceeds to Billets at PIERREGOT.	
	6/5/16		Do. In Billets at PIERREGOT.	
	7/5/16		Do.	
	8/5/16		Do.	
	9/5/16		Do.	
	10/5/16		Do.	
	11/5/16		Do.	
	12/5/16		Do.	
	13/5/16		Do.	
	14/5/16		Do.	

WAR DIARY
or
INTELLIGENCE SUMMARY
(Erase heading not required.)

Army Form C. 2118

Place	Date	Hour	Summary of Events and Information	Remarks and references to Appendices
PIERREGOT	15/5/16		In Billets at PIERREGOT.	
	16/5/16		Do.	
	17/5/16		The Battalion march into Billets at SENLIS.	
SENLIS	18/5/16		Battalion relieved 15th A.L.I in BLACK HORSE BRIDGE DUG-OUTS. Relief complete by 11-45pm.	
	19/5/16		In occupancy of BLACK HORSE BRIDGE DUG-OUTS. Other ranks wounded 2.	
	20/5/16		Do.	
	21/5/16		Do.	Other ranks wounded 2.
	22/5/16		Do.	
	23/5/16		Relieved 2nd K.O.Y.L.I. in THIEPVAL SUB-SECTOR. 17th A.L.I on right, 15th R.I.R on left.	
	24/5/16		Do.	Other ranks killed 1.
	25/5/16		Do.	
	26/5/16		Do.	Other ranks Wounded 7.
	27/5/16		The Battalion relieved by 2nd K.O.Y.L.I. Relief complete 10pm. The Battalion moved into DUG-OUTS at BLACK HORSE BRIDGE.	

Army Form C. 2118

WAR DIARY
or
INTELLIGENCE SUMMARY
(Erase heading not required.)

Place	Date	Hour	Summary of Events and Information	Remarks and references to Appendices
BLACKHORSE BRIDGE	28/5/16		In occupancy of Dug-outs at BLACKHORSE BRIDGE	w.o.f
	29/5/16		Do	w.o.f
	30/5/16		Battalion relieved by 2nd Innskilling relief complete 11-45 p.m and moved to Bivouacs at AVELUY WOOD	w.o.f
	31/5/16		Do	w.o.f

97th Brigade.
32nd Division.

1/16th BATTALION

HIGHLAND LIGHT INFANTRY

JUNE 1916

XXXII

To: D.A.G.,
General Headquarters,
3rd Echelon.

War Diary of the 16th (Service) Battalion The Highland Light Infantry for the period of 1/30th June. 1916., herewith.

K Simpson Lt & Adjt., for O.C.,
16th (Service) Bn. H.L.I.,

1st July 1916.

Volume 8 Page 1

WAR DIARY
or
INTELLIGENCE SUMMARY.
(Erase heading not required.)

Army Form C. 2118.

Instructions regarding War Diaries and Intelligence Summaries are contained in F. S. Regs., Part II. and the Staff Manual respectively. Title pages will be prepared in manuscript.

Hour, Date, Place		Summary of Events and Information	Remarks and references to Appendices
June, 1916	AVELUY WOOD	In Bivouacs AVELUY WOOD	Fine
2nd	"	Do	Fine
3rd	"	Do	Fine
4th	"	Do	Fine
5th	"	Do	Fine
6th	"	Do the following Officers joined the Battalion 2nd Lieut J. Lewis	Fine
7th	"	The Battalion moved into Bivouacs in MARTINSART WOOD	Fine
8th	MARTINSART WOOD	In Bivouacs in MARTINSART WOOD	Fine
9th	"	Do	Fine
10th	"	Do	Fine
11th	"	The Battalion moved into Billets in SENLIS	Fine
12th	SENLIS	In Billets in SENLIS	Fine
13th	"	The Battalion moved into Huts in CONTAY WOOD	Fine
14th	CONTAY WOOD	In Billets (Huts) in CONTAY WOOD	Fine

Volume 8 Page 2

Army Form C. 2118.

WAR DIARY
or
INTELLIGENCE SUMMARY.
(Erase heading not required.)

Instructions regarding War Diaries and Intelligence Summaries are contained in F. S. Regs., Part II. and the Staff Manual respectively. Title pages will be prepared in manuscript.

Hour, Date, Place		Summary of Events and Information	Remarks and references to Appendices
14th June, 1916	CONTAY WOOD	In Huts in CONTAY WOOD	
15th	"	Do	
16th	"	Do	
17th	"	Do	
18th	"	Do	
19th	"	Do	
20th	"	Do	
21st	"	Do	
22nd	"	Do	
22nd	SENLIS	The Battalion moved into Billets at SENLIS	
23rd	"	In Billets in SENLIS	
23rd	"	Do { The following Officers joined the Battalion 2nd Lieut. T.H. Miller, 2nd Lieut. M.A. Hamilton	
24th	"	Do { The following Officer joined the Battalion 2nd Lieut. A.M. Tweedy	
25th	"	Do	
26th	"	The Battalion moved into Bivouacs in MARTINSART WOOD	

Volume 8 page 3

WAR DIARY
or
INTELLIGENCE SUMMARY.

(Erase heading not required.)

Army Form C. 2118.

Instructions regarding War Diaries and Intelligence Summaries are contained in F.S. Regs., Part II. and the Staff Manual respectively. Title pages will be prepared in manuscript.

Hour, Date, Place	Summary of Events and Information	Remarks and references to Appendices
28th June, 1916 MARTINSART WOOD	In Bivouacs in MARTINSART WOOD. Killed in Action 2nd Lieutenant D.R. McDonnell, 2 Other Ranks, Wounded 8 Other ranks. Battalion moved from MARTINSART WOOD to Bivouacs in BOUZINCOURT at 7 P.m.	WDI
29th June, 1916 BOUZINCOURT	In Bivouacs in BOUZINCOURT.	WDI
30th June, 1916 Do.	Do. Killed 2 Other Ranks, Wounded 2 Other Ranks. The Battalion left BOUZINCOURT at 9.30pm to take up Battle position in AUTHUILLE SUBSECTOR between points R.31.a.74 and R.31.c.15	WDI

VOLUME: Page No. One.

Army Form C. 2118.

Instructions regarding War Diaries and Intelligence
Summaries are contained in F. S. Regs., Part II.
and the Staff Manual respectively. Title pages
will be prepared in manuscript.

WAR DIARY
or
~~INTELLIGENCE SUMMARY.~~

(Erase heading not required.)

Hour, Date, Place	Summary of Events and Information	Remarks and references to Appendices
	The 16th H.L.I. with 25 Officers and 755 other ranks, relieved the 2nd K.O.Y.L.I. on the night of 30th June/1st July, 1916, taking over from them the trench system extending from SKINNER STREET, point R.31.a.14., to TYNDRUM STREET, point R.31.c.05., (approximately 500 yards of front). Casualties during relief :- 1 Other Ranks killed ; 2 Other Ranks wounded.	See Appendix 1.
JULY, 1st.	Before midnight, Lieut. BOGUE and 2 other ranks reconnoitred the German Wire, and found that the wire was very much broken down, and that there were numerous gaps in it. They reported that they anticipated no difficulty in getting through the wire. During the whole night we bombarded the enemy's trenches heavily, to which he retaliated feebly. At 6-25 a.m. the bombardment prior to the advance commenced, and continued until ZERO Time at 7-30 a.m. During that time our front line and communication trenches were badly shelled with H.E., Shrapnel, and Minenwerfer. The advance commenced at 7-30 a.m. "A" Company leading on the right, with "C" Company in Support, and "B" Company on the left, with "D" Company in Support. On our right were the 17th H.L.I., and on our left the 16th North'd Fusrs. The 2nd K.O.Y.L.I. were in Support, and the 11th Border Regt. in Reserve. The enemy opened heavy Machine Gun and Rifle Fire as soon as our men jumped over the parapet, and manned their parados with bombers, with men at 2 yards interval. Our platoons advanced in waves in extended order, and were simply mown down by the Machine Gun Fire, and very heavy casualties resulted. On the left the Support Company got close up to the German wire, but were unable to advance. On the right we succeeded in entering the German Trenches, where we were in touch with the 17th H.L.I., and where we remained until relieved by the 2nd Manchesters.	See Appendix 2. Bn. Orders attached

VOLUME. PAGE TWO.

Army Form C. 2118.

Instructions regarding War Diaries and Intelligence
Summaries are contained in F. S. Regs., Part II.
and the Staff Manual respectively. Title pages
will be prepared in manuscript.

WAR DIARY
or
INTELLIGENCE SUMMARY.
(Erase heading not required.)

Hour, Date, Place	Summary of Events and Information	Remarks and references to Appendices
JULY, 1st.	On our left the men took what cover they could in Shell holes, firing upon the enemy whenever he showed himself. One of our Lewis Gunners fired 24 Magazines of Ammunition, when it was finished, being the only one of his section left he crawled back under cover of darkness, bringing the Gun with him. During the day all available men were organized into Bombing Posts, and were prepared to offer every resistance should the enemy have made any attempt to counter attack. The Artillery were informed of our position, and during the afternoon bombarded the front line opposite us very heavily. The Germans were very active with Machine Gun, Rifle Fire, Bombs and "Oil Cans" on "No Man's Land," sniping at any man who made any movement. In retaliation to our bombardment in the afternoon our trenches were heavily shelled. This decreased during the night, but was renewed again between 3 and 5 a.m. Numerous flares were sent up during the night, including many red and green. The enemy were very much on the alert, and kept "No Man's Land" under continuous fire. We were in touch with the 15th Lancashire Fusrs. on our left, and with the 2nd K.O.Y.L.I. on our right. Colonel Laidlaw having been wounded was evacuated about 8 a.m., and Major Kyle joined the Battalion and took over Command about 5 p.m. Our casualties during the day were 20 Officers, and 534 other ranks.	See Appendix 3. W.D.T.

VOLUME 9. PAGE THREE.

Army Form C. 2118.

WAR DIARY
or
INTELLIGENCE SUMMARY.

(Erase heading not required.)

Instructions regarding War Diaries and Intelligence Summaries are contained in F.S. Regs., Part II. and the Staff Manual respectively. Title pages will be prepared in manuscript.

Hour, Date, Place	Summary of Events and Information	Remarks and references to Appendices
JULY, 2nd.	About 1 a.m. we were reinforced by a detachment of the 17th H.L.I., Colonel Morton taking over Command of the troops in the Sector. The morning of July, 2nd. was quiet, although the enemy were very much on the XMA alert, and sniped continuously. In the afternoon there was heavy firing on our left and right, and between 3 and 6 p.m. we were heavily shelled. During the remainder of the evening there was intermittent shelling. About 6 p.m. reinforcements of 1 officer and 200 other ranks of the 11th Border Regt., reported.	W.D.J.
JULY, 3rd.	We were relieved by the 8th Border Regt., the relief being complete at 3-30 a.m. Our own trenches were very heavily shelled while it was taking place. The Battalion proceeded into Dug-outs at CRUCIFIX CORNER. The Battalion moved from CRUCIFIX Dug-outs at 10-30 p.m. to Hutments in CONTAY WOOD, arriving there at 2-30 a.m. on the 4th inst. Casualties : 1 Other Ranks wounded.	W.D.J.
JULY, 4th, 5th, 6th, 7th.	In Hutments CONTAY WOOD.	W.D.J.
JULY, 7th.	The Battalion moved from Hutments in CONTAY WOOD to Billets in SENLIS.	W.D.J.

VOLUME 9. PAGE FOUR.

Army Form C. 2118.

Instructions regarding War Diaries and Intelligence
Summaries are contained in F. S. Regs., Part II.
and the Staff Manual respectively. Title pages
will be prepared in manuscript.

WAR DIARY
or
INTELLIGENCE SUMMARY.
(Erase heading not required.)

Hour, Date, Place	Summary of Events and Information	Remarks and references to Appendices
JULY, 8th.	In Billets in SENLIS. The Battalion moved from Billets in SENLIS to AVELUY BRIDGE HEAD DEFENCES, arriving there 11-50 p.m.	W.D.J.
JULY, 9th.	In occupation AVELUY BRIDGE HEAD DEFENCES (Crucifix Corner Dug--outs).	W.D.J.
JULY, 10th.	The Battalion relieved the 17th H.L.I. in QUARRY POST, NAB Sub-Sector, relief complete 3-30 p.m. Battalion in Support. Casualties : 1 other ranks killed in Action., 8 other ranks wounded.	W.D.J.
JULY, 11th.	In Occupation QUARRY POST. Casualties : 1 Other Ranks killed, 2 other ranks wounded.	W.D.J.
JULY, 12th.	In occupation QUARRY POST. Casualties : 2 other ranks wounded. 16th H.L.I. relieved 2nd K.O.Y.L.I. in NAB Sub-Sector. Relief complete by 5-30 p.m.	W.D.J.
JULY, 13th.	In occupation NAB Sub-Sector.	W.D.J.
JULY, 14th.	In occupation NAB Sub-Sector. Casualties : 1 other ranks wounded.	W.D.J.

VOLUME PAGE FIVE.

Army Form C. 2118.

Instructions regarding War Diaries and Intelligence
Summaries are contained in F.S. Regs., Part II.
and the Staff Manual respectively. Title pages
will be prepared in manuscript.

WAR DIARY
or
INTELLIGENCE SUMMARY.

(Erase heading not required.)

Hour, Date, Place	Summary of Events and Information	Remarks and references to Appendices
JULY, 15th.	In occupation NAB Sub-Sector. The Battalion was relieved by the 6th K.O.Y.L.I., relief complete by 10 p.m., and proceeded to Billets in BOUZINCOURT.	W.J.
JULY, 16th,	In Billets, BOUZINCOURT. The Battalion moved from Billets in BOUZINCOURT to Hutments in AMPLIERS. Route : ACHEUX, SARTON.	W.J.
JULY, 17th.	In Hutments, AMPLIERS. The Battalion moved from Hutments in AMPLIERS to Billets in SUS-ST-LEGER. Route : HALLOY, LUCHEUX. The undernoted Officers joined the Battalion for duty :- 2nd Lieut. J. Miller. 2nd Lieut. J. R. C. Phillips. 2nd Lieut. E. Mullen. 2nd Lieut. G. W. Campbell.	W.J.
JULY, 18th.	In Billets, SUS-ST-LEGER.	W.J.
JULY, 19th.	In Billets, SUS-ST-LEGER. The Battalion moved from Billets in SUS-ST-LEGER to Billets in MAISNIL ST. POL. Route : BEAUDRICOURT, ETREE WAMIN, HOUVIN HOUVIGNEUL.	W.J.
JULY, 20th.	In Billets, MAISNIL ST. POL. The Battalion moved from Billets in MAISNIL ST. POL. to Billets in HESTRUS. Route : ROELLECOURT, OSTREVILLE, BRYAS.	W.J.

VOLUME 9. PAGE SIX.

Army Form C. 2118.

WAR DIARY
or
INTELLIGENCE SUMMARY.
(Erase heading not required.)

Instructions regarding War Diaries and Intelligence Summaries are contained in F.S. Regs., Part II. and the Staff Manual respectively. Title pages will be prepared in manuscript.

Hour, Date, Place	Summary of Events and Information	Remarks and references to Appendices

JULY, 21st	In Billets, HESTRUS. The Battalion moved from Billets in HESTRUS to Billets in ALLOUAGNE. Route : TANGRY, PERNES, AUCHEL. The undernoted Officers joined the Battalion for Duty :—
	     2nd Lieut. F. G. Harris.
	     2nd Lieut. D. A. Milholm.
	     2nd Lieut. A. J. Senders.
		w.o.t.
		 w.o.t.

JULY, 22nd.	In Billets, ALLOUAGNE.	

JULY, 23rd.	In Billets, ALLOUAGNE. The undernoted Officers joined the Battalion for duty :—
	     2nd Lieut. H. A. Agnew.
	     2nd Lieut. R. G. A. Temple.
	     2nd Lieut. J. Stewart.
	     2nd Lieut. M. M. Lyon.
	 1 Other ranks accidentally wounded.
		w.o.t.

JULY, 24th.	In Billets, ALLOUAGNE.	w.o.t.
JULY, 25th.	In Billets, ALLOUAGNE.	w.o.t.
JULY, 26th.	In Billets, ALLOUAGNE. The Battalion moved from Billets in ALLOUAGNE to Billets in BETHUNE. Route : ALLOUAGNE, CHOCQUES. In Billets, BETHUNE.	w.o.t.
July, 27th, 28th, 29th, 30th. 31st. 2	In Billets, BETHUNE.	w.o.t.

R. Hayle Lieut-Col
Commanding 16th H.L.I.

APPENDICES 1, 2 & 3.

APPENDIX. 1.

16th (Service) Battalion H.L.I.

LIST OF OFFICERS WHO WENT INTO ACTION WITH THE BATTALION ON 1st JULY, 1916.

Headquarters :

Lieut. Col. & Hon. Col.	D. Laidlaw,	Commanding.
Captain	W. D. Scott,	Adjutant.
2nd Lieut.	A. C. Smith,	Intelligence Officer.
2nd Lieut.	A. P. Wilson,	Lewis Gun and Liaison Officer.
2nd Lieut.	A. McFarlane,	Officer i/c Mopping Party.
Lieut.	V. E. Badcock.	Medical Officer.

"A" COMPANY :

Captain D. B. Kerr.
2nd Lieut. R. A. Bogue.
   do.   R. Mitchell.
   do.   J. Kerr.
   do.   G. McCurrach.

"B" COMPANY :

Captain G. S. Fraser.
2nd Lieut. R. S. Brown.
   do.   J. A. Brown.
   do.   P. S. Hodgkinson.

"C" COMPANY :

Major J. McElwain.
Lieut. W. McLaren.
2nd Lieut. J. A. Gemmill.
   do.   J. Laing.
   do.   D. S. McHardy.

"D" COMPANY :

Captain F. W. Reid.
Lieut. T. Johnson.
2nd Lieut. J. Murdoch.
   do.   R. B. Stewart.
   do.   J. Cooper.

Wm. D. Scott

Captain & Adjutant,
16th (Service) Battalion H.L.I.,

31st July, 1916.

APPENDIX "A"

REGIMENTAL SECTOR:-	X.1.a.5.9. - R.ANCRE. Held by the 99th Res. Regt. of the 26th Res. Div., 14th Res. Corps. The 109th Res. Regt. hold the Sector South of this.
Battalion Boundary:-	R.25. central.
Regimental H.Q.:-	COURCELETTE at R.30.a.5.4.
Battalion H.Q. (Right)	ST PIERRE DIVION, in Reserve lines: large dug-out beside road at Q.24.b.80.95.
Battalion H.Q. (Left)	Reserve line at R.31.b.25.25.
Battalion H.Q. (when resting)	COURCELETTE R.30.a.95.90.
Company H.Q.:-	(1) West of THIEPVAL at R.25.d.05.92. (2) Support Co. about R.19.d.40.60.
Regimental Rest Billets:-	COURCELETTE.
M.G. Co. Transport and Rest Billets	GREVILLERS.
Command Posts:-	MOUQUET FARM or R.27.b.0.4.
Method of holding line:-	Two battalions in front line & support. 1 Battalion in Rest billets at COURCELETTE. 1 Battalion in Divisional Reserve.
Routes to Trenches:-	(1) COURCELETTE to MOUQUET FARM, thence by communication trenches. (2) COURCELETTE (?) via GRANDCOURT to ST PIERRE DIVION: thence by communication trenches.
Supply Dumps:-	(1) Pioneer Dump S.E. corner of COURCELETTE. (2) Pioneer and Ration Dump, Eastern end of THIEPVAL (ammunition also dumped here). (3) Ration dump and Kitchens in Reserve line at R.19.d.80.50. (4) GRANDCOURT.
Ammunition Dumps:-	THIEPVAL FARM - also Grenade store.
Telephones:-	Telephone Exchange at MOUQUET FARM.
Water Supply:-	Pipe lines into COURCELETTE. From there by water carts to THIEPVAL. This supply is supplemented by well near Church in THIEPVAL.
Railways:-	From COURCELETTE Pioneer Park to THIEPVAL Pioneer Park.
Railhead:-	LE SARS ?

HOSTILE ARTILLERY OPPOSITE 32ND DIVISION FRONT.

SITUATION.	NUMBER & NATURE OF BATTERY.
POZIERES	(6 77 mm.
	(1 10.5 cm.
	(1 15 cm.
R.21.b.28.22.	1 77 mm Battery
R.21.a.55.60.	- do -
R.27.b.43.13.	- do -
R.28.a.20.70.	- do -
R.28.c.90.00.	- do -
R.28.c.95.50.	- do -
R.33.b.20.23.	- do -
R.34.a.97.64. to) R.34.b.20.45.)	- do -
R.15.c.52.50.	- do -
R.15.d.02.70.	- do -
R.15.b.35.30.	1 15 cm.
R.15.b.38.60.	1 10.5 cm.

PARTICULARS OF ROADS BEHIND THE GERMAN LINES.

From information obtained from Refugees.

THIEPVAL-AUTHUILLE.

Metalled road, about 5 metres wide in all. Metalling 3 metres road.

THIEPVAL-HAMEL.

Metalled. About 5 metres wide. Crosses the R. ANCRE by a brick bridge.

THIEPVAL-POZIERES

5 metres wide (metalled) A 12 foot road leads from it to the FERME DE MOUQUET at Point R.33.a.4.4.

THIEPVAL-GRANDCOURT

Good metalled road, 5 metres wide, 3 metres metalled.

OVILLERS-GRANDCOURT

A cart track (Unmetalled). Leaves OVILLERS N. and passes the THIEPVAL-POZIERES road in R.32.b.

FERME DE MOUQUET-GRANDCOURT

Road unmetalled to R.22.a., thence metalled to GRANDCOURT.

PARTICULARS OF WELLS IN VILLAGES BEHIND THE GERMAN LINES.

From information obtained from Refugees.

THIEPVAL.

There are 3 wells (communales), depth about 30 metres, containing good water, which may be now polluted. There are also wells to be found in most of the farm houses.

FERME DE MOUQUET

The farm contains several wells. There is a pipe line from the FERME DE MOUQUET to THIEPVAL.

THIEPVAL.

There are 66 houses in THIEPVAL, chiefly farms. Most of these have rain water cisterns.

The Chateau, facing West, is an important building the cellars of which are very large and are used by the Germans for lodging soldiers, and are always full.

THIEPVAL farm is used as a grenade store.

The village is in ruins but from latest reports and from aeroplane photographs it may be deduced that many of its less fragile buildings are still so little damaged as to afford valuable protection against attack.

The following are a few particulars of the buildings that may have escaped our gun fire. The rest may be taken as mere flimsy barns of "torches" (unbaked clay and chopped straw).:-

1. GRIBEAUVAL farm. Brick, some cellarage - say 20 men.
2. Maison MORONVAL. A small brick house with cellars for 15 men.
3. Maison OBIN. A "torches" house which, however, has been sandbagged by the Germans, and has good cellars which are protected by barrels of earth. A small fort for about 40 men.
4. Maison CATHELAIN. A large strongly built house (brick) of seven rooms. Its cellars will hold about 50 men and the whole has been fortified.
5. Maison BARNS which has been strengthened by the enemy.
6. Maison The Cures house (presbytery). A substantial little building of brick with cellars in which 62 people lived for 40 days.
7. Maison SOREL. A small farm with indifferent cellarage.
8. Maison BENJAMIN. A brick house with excellent cellars capable of holding 40-50 men.
9. A sandbagged farm.
10. Maison BAUDELOQUE. A poor house which has been fortified. It has cellars for 10-15 men.
11. Maison DARCHEZ. A "torches" farm with cellars for 20-30 men. It has a good well.
12. A cafe burnt down in 1915. Excellent cellars 30-40 men.
13. A small house with a good well.

Tower in THIEPVAL WOOD, 300 metres North of the Chateau and 80 metres S.S.W. of HAIE, the most Westerly building on the THIEPVAL-St. PIERRE DIVION road and North of it, is loopholed and contains an O.P.

It is estimated that there is accommodation for 1500 men underground.

There are 3 wells (communales), depth about 30 metres, containing good water. There are also wells to be found in most of the farm houses. The water supply of the Chateau is considered abundant. The well in the square North of the Church was mined and had a gallery running towards the Church.

There is a deep, walled-in village pond.

<u>Telephones.</u>   Behind a wall on the Eastern side of the square by the Church.

APPENDIX 'A' (CONT'D)

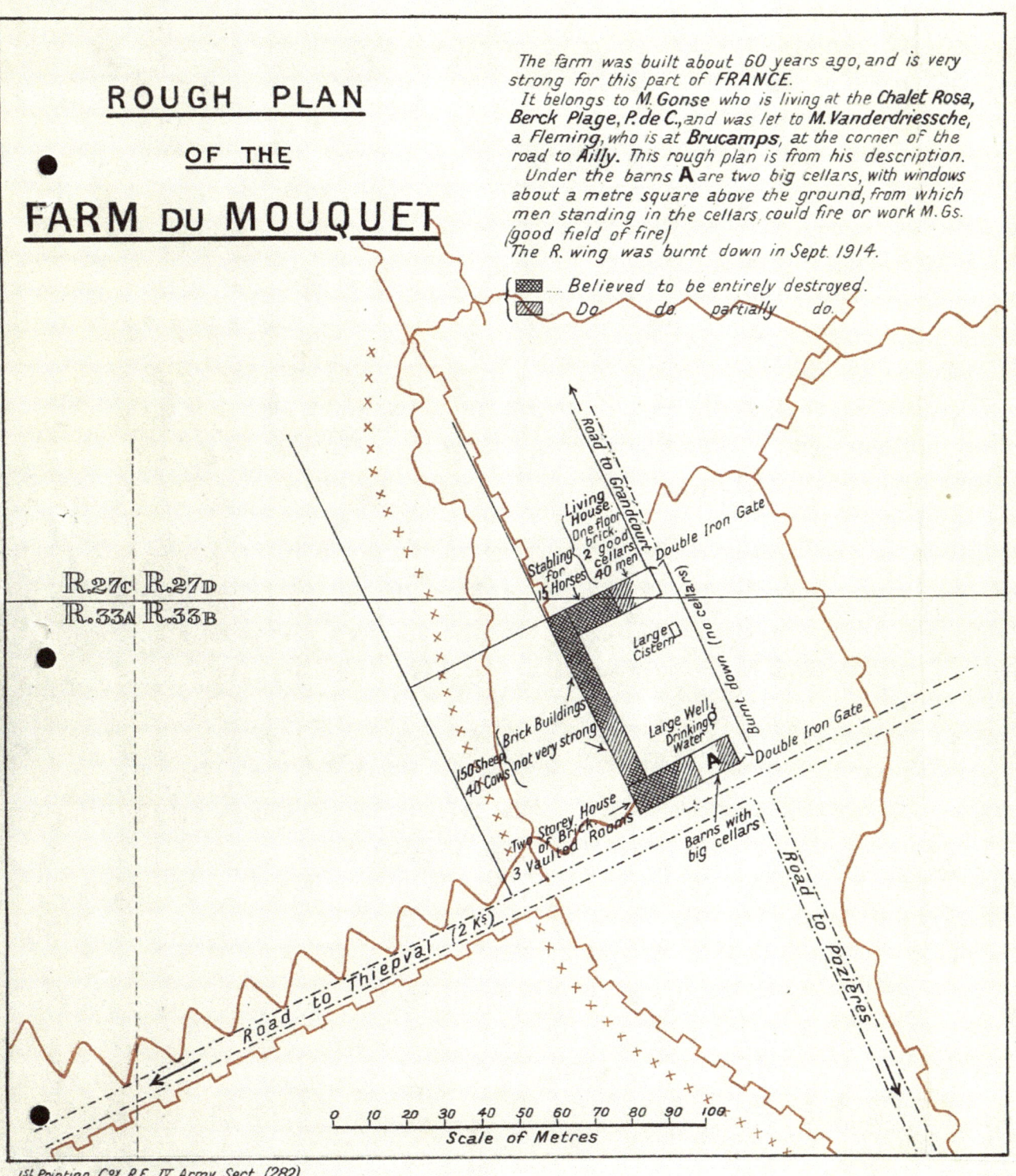

FERME DE MOUQUET.

A large farm belonging to a Belgian.

There are 2 supply dumps and an Artillery dump in it or its vicinity.

There is a pipe line from the FERME DE MOUQUET to THIEPVAL.

The farm contains several wells.

The telephone exchange is situated here.

Under the two barns are 4 big cellars, with windows about a metre square above the ground, from which men standing in the cellars could fire or work Machine Guns (good field of fire). The cellars are capable of holding 40 men.

The Right wing was burnt down in Sept. 1914.

There are several small clusters of trees N., N.W., S.W. and S. of the farm in which batteries are placed.

97th Infantry Brigade   Programme of Moves

Day.	Battalion	Location of 1st Line Transport		March Routes. TIMES
S.	11th Border R. 2nd K.O.Y.L.I. 16th H.L.I. 17th H.L.I.	CONTAY and CONTAY WOOD		**Night S/T.** 11th Border R. main road to BOUZINCOURT to reach there by 11p.m. 2nd K.O.Y.L.I. and 16th H.L.I. to SENLIS and 17th H.L.I. to WARLOY all to be in Billets by 12.30 a.m.
T.	11th Border R. 2nd K.O.Y.L.I. 16th H.L.I. 17th H.L.I.	BOUZINCOURT BOUZINCOURT SENLIS SENLIS WARLOY	SENLIS SENLIS WARLOY	**Night T/U** 2nd K.O.Y.L.I. 11th Border R. by main road BOUZINCOURT and AVELUY, to clear BOUZINCOURT by 11 p.m.
U, V, and W.	11th Border R 2nd K.O.Y.L.I. 16th H.L.I. 17th H.L.I.	In LINE CRUCIFIX CORNER SENLIS SENLIS	BOUZINCOURT Do. SENLIS SENLIS	**Night W/X** 2nd K.O.Y.L.I. enter Line & 11th Border R. withdraw to CRUCIFIX CORNER
X.	2nd K.O.Y.L.I. 11th Border R 16th H.L.I. 17th H.L.I.	IN LINE CRUCIFIX CORNER SENLIS SENLIS	BOUZINCOURT Do. SENLIS SENLIS	**Night X/Y** 16th H.L.I. and 17th H.L.I. P. Road. Transport by main roads. To be clear of SENLIS by Midnight and behind 14th Bde Units, last unit of which clears SENLIS by 11.30p.m.
Y.	2nd K.O.Y.L.I. 11th Border R. 17th H.L.I. 16th H.L.I.	IN LINE CRUCIFIX CORNER V.24-W13 XXXX W.14-15	BOUZINCOURT Do. BOUZINCOURT Do.	**Y/Z Night** 16th H.L.I. and 17th H.L.I. by P. Road-PIONEER ROAD-BROOKERS PASS to be clear of River ANCRE by 10.30p.m. 2nd K.O.Y.L.I. occupy Battle position KINTYRE STREET 11th Border R. occupy Battle position AUTHUILLE WOOD. 16th H.L.I. occupy Battle position in left of Line 17th H.L.I. occupy Battle position in Right of Line ---- 2 Battalions 96th Bde by P road -PIONEER ROAD-BLACKHORSE ROAD to follow 97th Bde.
Z.	97th Bde. all up in RIGHT	All in open N.W. and S.E. of BOUZINCOURT VILLAGE		

APPENDIX H.1.

ALLOCATION OF TRENCHES TO BATTALIONS
PRIOR TO ATTACK

			"A"	"B"
Brigade Frontage			"A"	"B"
Front Line	2 Platoons "A" & "B" Coys		1. Coy	1. Coy
Second Line.	(Bisset Trench) (Durham Street)	2 Platoons "A" & "B" Coys	1. Coy.	1. Coy
Third Line	(Kilmun Street) (Tarbert Street) (Davaar Avenue) (Ardrishaig St) (Campbell Avenue) (Oban Avenue)	2 Platoons "C" & "D" Coys	1. Coy	1. Coy (or in TOBERMORY STREET)
TOBERMORY STREET	= 2 Platoons "C" & "D" Coys		1. Coy	
Extension Of DURHAM STREET and CHOWBENT STREET				1. Coy
KINTYRE STREET and Communicating trenches with TOBERMORY STREET and AUTHUILLE			Support Battalion	
Trenches in AUTHUILLE WOOD			Reserve Battalion	

HEADQUARTERS :-

"A" Battalion   Dug-Out Leading off THIEPVAL AVENUE

"B" Battalion   CAMPBELL POST

"C" Battalion   Dug-Out close to CAMPBELL AVENUE

"D" BATtalion   AUTHUILLE WOOD TRENCHES.

APPENDIX B. 1.

PROGRAMME OF PRELIMINARY BOMBARDMENT.

		SPECIAL
V. Day	Bombardment all day and at intervals during the night. Concentration of fire and intermittent fire on enemy billets.	concentrated from 4 p.m. to 5.20 p.m.
W. Day	As for V Day	concentrated from 9 a.m. to 10.20 a.m.
X. Day	As for V Day	concentrated from 4.30 a.m. to 5.50 a.m. and again from 6.30 p.m. to 7 p.m.
Y. Day	As for V Day	concentrated from 6 a.m. to 7.20 a.m. and from 4 p.m. to 5.20 p.m.
Z. Day	Concentrated from -65' mins. to Zero, subsequently as per Corps Programme. Hurricane Bombardment by 3" Stokes just prior to the assault	

NOTES

1. Counter-Battery work very active throughout.

2. Wire Cutting commences on U Day, and continues to Y. Day.

3. The Heavy Howitzers may cease firing during a certain period every day in order to permit of photography and verification of fire.

4. Bombardment of billets by day and night :-

   (a) Sudden concentration of fire, e.g. for a few minutes, 10 to 15 minutes subsequent to discharge of gas.

   (b) Intermittent bursts of fire on billets and approaches, especially at night.

5. The shelling of communications, approaches, paths, railways, working parties, etc., with the object of preventing replenishment of ammunition, food and water, demands co-operation of Field Artillery, Machine Guns and rifles on an inner zone.

6. At Zero on Z Day, the artillery will lift off the Front trenches and the infantry will deliver the assault.
   The Hour of Zero will be notified to Corps on W or X Days.

7. Our trenches during U - Y Days to be kept as empty as possible, especially during the discharge of gas and smoke.

The Programme of preliminary Bombardment (Appendix B.1.) has been amended as follows :-
(a) On V. Day there will be no bombardment, but only registration, concentration of fire on enemy's billets, and intermittent fire during the night.
(B) The special concentrated bombardment from 6.30 p.m. to 7 p.m. on X day and from 4 p.m. to 5.20 p.m. on Y Day are cancelled.

APPENDIX B.2

Table of Lifts for 18 pdr Batteries

Table of Lifts of 18 pdr Batteries to be read in conjunction with map of Artillery Lifts - APPENDIX B.2. - Copied by Units' representatives to-day

The Frontal Barrage leaves the line "A" and moves to "B" at 0 - 0'
Enfilade Barrage leaves the line "A" .. .. "B" at 0- 22
                                                        - 45
The Barrage leaves the line   "B" .. .. "C" at 3 - 0
    Do.   Do.   "C" .. .. "D" at 18- 0
    Do.   Do.   "D" .. .. "E" at 28 -0
    Do.   Do.   "E" .. .. "F" at 52- 0
    Do.   Do.   "F" .. .. "G" at 1-18-0
    Do..   Do.   "G" .. .. "I" at 1-35-0

Appendix Z (19 Pages)

SECRET.

War Diary

23rd June, 1916.

16th (Service) Battalion H.L.I.

OPERATION ORDER No. 1.

Reference :-Sheet 57.d.S.E., Scale 1/20,000.

1. The 32nd Division is to take a principal part in an attack on the German positions.

Information. 2. The available information indicates no increase in the strength of the enemy opposite us. Details as to the enemy's strength, disposition and Artillery, are given in Appendix "A"

Intention. 3. It is the intention of the G.O.C., to attack the enemy with the utmost vigour and determination.

Objectives. 4. The objectives allotted to the Division are :-

(a) German Front System between R.32.c.0.0. and R.25.b.2.6.

(b) German Intermediate system and MOUQUET Switch between R.33.b.0.3. and R.20.c.8.2.

(c) German 2nd Line System between R.34.a.0.9. and R.21.c.1.7.

Neighbour 5. The 8th and 36th Divisions will simultaneously attack on
:ing Divisions our Right and Left respectively.

6. There will be a steady bombardment by our guns day and night for four days up to the moment of assault on the fifth day, (Z) day.
On the day before this bombardment begins, the Artillery will commence to cut the enemy's wire with shrapnel and 2" mortars. Rifle and M.G. fire will be kept up each night during the bombardment to prevent the enemy repairing his wire.
Programme of Lifts are given in Appendices B.1. and B.2.

7.
Preliminary (a) The 16th H.L.I. will move in accordance with
Moves and Appendix, Programme of Moves, and on the night X/Z
Sequence of will take up Battle Position in accordance with
Events. Appendix H.1.

8.
Cutting Such wire in our trenches as is required to be removed to
our Wire. facilitate our attack, will be dealt with gradually by Units in the line, prior to the nigh Y/Z, Gaps being marked as required by boards already issued. The front line wire will be cut by the 2nd K.O.Y.L.I. on the night X/Y in diagonal strips, the loose wire being thrown over the uncut strips.

9.
Infantry (a) The assult of the first and second objectives will be carried
Tasks. out by the 96th and 97th Infantry Brigades.

(b) The assult of the 96th and 97th Infantry Brigades will be delivered by two assulting columns in each Brigade, each column being composed of 1 Battalion, formed up in depth on a front of two Platoons.

(c) The objectives of the 97th Infantry Brigade will be :-

1. The German Front System from X.1.a.6.8. to R.31.a.50.45.

2. The line R.31.d.8.1. - R.32.c.3.7. - R.26.c.3.1.

3. The line R.33.a.7R.5. - R.27.c.25.75.

2. O.O. No.1.

Infantry Tasks Contd.

9. 4. FERME DU MOUQUET and trenches encircling it, and MOUQUET SWITCH to R.27.c.25.75.

10. (b) In accordance with paras. 9. (a), (b), and (c) the assault will be carried out at Zero time on "Z" day by the 16th and 17th High.L.I. leading (on the LEFT and Right respectively) the 2nd K.O.Y.L.I. in SUPPORT and the 11th Border Regt., echeloned to the RIGHT rear of the RIGHT leading Regiment, in reserve.

The 16th High.L.I. and 17th High.L.I. will capture the first three objectives mentioned in the foregoing Battalion Order para. 9 (c), moving forward in accordance with the Artillery barrages, (Appendix B.2. and Map copied by Units.) On the above objectives being captured, the 11th Border Regt. on the RIGHT, and 2nd K.O.Y.L.I. on the LEFT will pass through the 16th and 17th High.L.I. and capture the fourth objective in accordance with the Artillery barrages.

The RIGHT of the 16th High.L.I will direct – Bearing 69 degrees True Bearing, which passes the edge of the S.E. Corner of FORT WUNDERWERK. True bearing of left of 16th High.L.I. is 71.30. and true Bearing on right of 17th High.LII. is 67 degrees.

RIGHT and LEFT flanks of the 97th Infantry Brigade attack are shewn by lines on Map B.2. (Copied by representatives of Units.

(c) Chief Artillery barrages and timing in attack, as in appendix "B.2."

(e) The 14th Infantry Brigade will follow the 97th Infantry Brigade, moving up the valley leading from the NAB, towards FERME DU MOUQUET, and will attack the 3rd objective referred to in para 4.

The 14th Infantry Brigade, after penetrating the German second Line, will then attack the remainder of the 3rd objective from the point of entry, i.e., from flank and rear. This 3rd objective will be consolidated and held by them.

Strong Points.

11. The 2nd K.O.Y.L.I. will detail one Company to consolidate strong points at :-
(A) R.31.d.85.35.   Garrison 1 Platoon with 1 Vickers Gun.
(A) R.31.d.9.8.   Garrison 1 Platoon with 1 Vickers Gun.

Two Platoons will remain as Garrisons, the other two after dumping R.E. material as arranged, will join their Units

The O.C. 97th Brigade M.G. Company, will direct 1 Vickers Gun to each strong point as soon as consolidation has commenced.

The 2nd K.O.Y.L.I. will also detail a Company to consolidate strong points at :-

(B) R.32.a.2.6.   Garrison 1 Platoon with 1 Vickers Gun.
(B) R.26.c.0.0.   Garrison 1 Platoon with 1 Vickers Gun.

Two Platoons will remain as Garrisons, the other two, after dumping R.E. material as arranged, will rejoin their Unit.

The O.C. 97th Brigade M.G. Company, will direct 1 Vickers Gun to each strong point as soon as consolidation has commenced.

3. O.O. No. 1.

Strong Points. 11. The 11th Border Regt. will detail one Company to consolidate strong points at :-
- (Y) R.33.a.6.4.   Garrison, 1 Platoon with 1 Vickers Gun.
- (Z) R.27.c.4.2.   Garrison, 1 Platoon with 1 Vickers Gun.
- (X) R.27.c.3.7.   Garrison, 1 Platoon with 2 Lewis Guns.

Three Platoons will remain as Garrisons, the remaining Platoon will rejoin its Unit after dumping R.E. Material.

Two Lewis Guns will form part of the Garrison at R.27.c. 3.7.
The O.C. 97th Brigade M.G. Company, will detail 1 Vickers Gun to be with each Garrison at -
R.33.a.6.4. and
R.27.c.4.2.

The 11th Border Regt will detail 1 Company to consolidate a strong Point at the FERME DU MOUQUET, and to act as Garrison with two Lewis Guns. O.C. 97th Brigade M.G. Company will detail two Vickers Guns to be with the Garrison also.

One section of 219th Field Company will be attached to 97th Infantry Brigade, and as arranged by O.C. Company will assist in preliminary work of consolidation, of the various strong points. The consolidating party of the 2nd K.O.Y.L.I. and the 11th Border Regt. will obtain and carry forward R.E. Materials under instructions already issued.

Mopping Parties. 12. These will be detailed as arranged, and work in accordance with circular already issued by the Brigade. When their task is completed, O.C. Moppers will detail two Parties of 1 N.C.O. and 25 men each to act as Grenade Carriers, and to report to Lieut. BLACKIE, Brigade Bombing Officer, at CAMPBELL POST. Prisoners conducted back by Moppers to the O.C. Moppers in "No Man's Lane" or by other escorts, will be taken straight to the divisional collecting station at BLACK HORSE BRIDGE, on EAST bank of River ANCRE.

Ammonal Parties. 13. A Party of each Company of the Brigade will carry two 9' lengths of Ammonal Torpedoes. These will be dumped at the S.A.A. Store in AUTHUILLE WOOD, lying in the 2b Trench Mortar Magazines, marked R.E. Magazines. Battalions on their way to their battle positions will send their Ammonal Parties with an Officer to draw them.

Corps. Reserve. 14. The 49th Division in Corps Reserve, is occupying a position of assembly in AVELUY WOOD on night Y/Z, and after 14th INF. Brigade moves, will be moved across River ANCRE and our present front line.

Time of Assault 15. The exact time for assault will be fixed by a higher authority. Zero will be the moment at which the Artillery lifts off the enemy's front line trench. At Zero, the leading Infantry must be as near the enemy's front line as our barrage permits, i.e. about 100 yards.

16. As soon as the attacking lines have crossed "No man's Land," the Russian Saps will be opened by R.E's for communication forward.

Gas. 17. (a) Gas Cylinders are being placed in special emplace : : ments in the front line between CHOWBENT STREET and

4. O.O. No. 4.

Gas 17 (a) SAUCHIEHALL STREET. The gas will be discharged on a day and at a time to be decided by higher authority. The noise of initial discharge of the gas will be covered by rapid rifle and machine gun fire all along the line. Gas Helmets of Units in the trenches will be inspected by Officers daily, after the Cylinders have been carried up.

(b) Smoke will be employed prior to the day of the assault to induce the enemy to man his parapets, when a heavy Artillery and Machine Gun Fire will be directed on them. The detailed arrangements for this smoke discharge will be notified later to all concerned.

(c) No. 1 Company, No. 5 Battalion, Special Brigade R.E. with 4" Stokes Mortars will be employed to form smoke barrages on the day of assult as follows :-
(1) To screen movement of our right assaulting column from enemy trenches, on the SOUTH SIDE of the valley, running from the NAB towards FERME DU MOUQUET, and at the same time to screen movement of the left assaulting column of the 8th Division from the enemy trenches from X.1.a.6.8. along X.1.b., and from R.31.d.3.0. to R.31.d.9.5. Barrage to be effective from minus 5' and to contine till plus 5' along the trenches as far as X.1.a.10.8. and thence EAST until plus 10'

(d) The arrangements for the discharge of Gas and for use of smoke are dependent on weather conditions.

Dress. 18.(a) Packs and Greatcoats will not be taken to the forming up positions on the night preceding the assault. On Y day, all packs and greatcoats will be stored by Brigades as under
  97th Bde., less 2 Battalions at AVELUY.
  Other Battalions, 97th Bde., at BOUZINCOURT.

Brigade Headquarters will detail 1 man to each dump to remain with packs and greatcoats left behind.

(b) Each Infantryman will carry
  Rifle and Equipment (less pack).
    (Water bottles FULL)
  2 Bandoliers of S.A.A. in addition to Equipment Ammunition (220 rounds in all). Bombers will carry Equipment ammunition only.
  Waterproof Sheet.
  2 Sandbags in belt.
  Unexpended portion of day's rations.
  One Iron (emergency) Ration.
  One 1-lb. Tin of Meat and Biscuits.

(c) Each Officer, N.C.O. and man of Infantry Battalions, including Pioneers, will carry two fused Mills Grenades in his pockets - except in the case of Bombers - These Grenades are not for use by the carriers ; they are intended as a means of getting forward large numbers of grenades, which will be collected as soon as the objectives are reached, so as to replenish the Bomber's Stocks.

(d) Wire Cutters and breakers will be issued by R.E. to Units prior to taking up Battle positions

(e) 200 red flares for communication with the Contact Patrol Aeroplane will be carried by each Battalion.

Trench Traffic Arrangements. 19. KILMUN STREET will be used as an UP trench, and KILBERRY STREET as a DOWN trench. The rule of the road does not apply to Staff Officers, Linesmen, and Messengers.

Transport 20. (b) On Z day, all echeloned "A" of 1st line Transport, viz., limbered G.S. Wagons for Machine Guns, Tools, S.A.A., *Water Carts.* Maltese Carts, (Medical* pack animals and Officers Mess Carts, will be brigaded under a selected Officer of each and will be prepared to move forward to the

5.   O.O. No. 1.

Transport	20. (b) space SOUTH of Pioneer Road, between W.16.a.8.6. and ~~W.16.b.XXXIX~~ W.16.b.5.6.

(c) The authorised establishment of baggage and stores including Officer Kits (35 lbs) will be packed in the Baggee Wagons of Units on X day

Police and Prisoners.   21. (a) Stragglers Posts will be established at
(1) Q.36.c.9.1.   (CAMPBELL AVENUE).
(2) W.5.b.9.12.   (BLACK HORSE BRIDGE).
(3) W.11.d.7.5.   (AVELU-AUTHUILLE ROAD).
(4) W.11.d.8.1.   (CRUCIFIX CORNER).

(b) (1) Prisoners will be sent under Escort to the Divisional Prisoner Collecting Station at BLACK HORSE BRIDGE, left bank of River ANCRE. Escorts must see that prisoners do not destroy documents.
(2) All information will be handed over by the Escort to the Officer i/c the Divisional Collecting Station, as to where and by whom the prisoners were captured.
All Documents will be collected and a preliminary and rapid examination made.
(3) Escort to prisoners will not exceed 1 man to 10 Prisoners.

Areas.   22. Area of Trench occupied by 16th H.L.I. prior to attack.
1. East Boundary, R.31.c.09.47 - R.31.a.10.27
2. South   -do-   R.31.c.09.47 - R.36.c.78.20
3. West   -do-   Q.36.c.78.20 - Q.36.d.25.80
4. North   -do-   Q.36.d.25.80 - R.31.a.10.27

KINTYRE TRENCH AND CAITHNESS STREET exclusive.

Miscellaneous Instructions.   23. (A). All Papers and Orders are to be destroyed before the advance. No papers will be carried by Officers and men taking part in the attack except the 1/20,000 Trench Map shewing the German Trenches only, the 1/40,000 Map, sheet 57.D., and 57.C. and the LENS sheet of the 1/100,000 series. All messages and reports will refer to one or other of those Maps.

(B) Men in the trenches and in the assaulting Brigades will not fall out to bring back wounded.

(C) Any Guns captured, which are in danger of being lost again, must be rendered useless by damaging the sights and breech mechanism. Captured Machine Guns must be collected.
The O.R.A. will have Teams ready to go forward to bring back captured guns.

(D) Attention is drawn to the orders already issued forbidding the collection of Souvenirs.

Veterinary.   24. A Veterinary Collecting Station will be established at W.13.a.2.8.

Stores.   25. The following Stores from the 219th Field Coy. R.E. Dump, BOUZINCOURT, will be drawn on X/Y night by the 16th High.L.I.

2 Grenades per man.
2 sandbags per man.
Wire Cutters Mark V.........   18
Longhandled 14"   14
S.A. Decimal................   80
Wire Breakers   64

6. O.O. No. 6

Water Arrangements on night of X/Y.	26. Transport of all Units will draw from 219th Field Coy. BOUZINCOURT, 4 cradles for carrying water on Mules, and from BOUZINCOURT COAL DUMP (W.7.c.4.0) they will draw the necessary number of two Gallon Petrol Tins. The cradles should hold 3 two gallon Petrol Tins per side. i.e., 6 per mule. These Petrol Tins are to be taken forward on Pack Animals full when they move forward for the first bound to space SOUTH of PIONEER road between W.16.a.8.6 and W.16.b.5.6
Reporting of Casualties in Action.	27. Estimated Return which will shew round numbers without distinction between killed, wounded or missing. (a) Officers by separate ranks (no names) (b) Other ranks. O.C. Companies will render return one hour after the commencement of attack, and also at the completion of the operation in hand. Accurate Return. Returns will be rendered to Battalion Headquarters at 2-30 p.m. and 5-30 a.m. daily during the operations.
Transport Lines.	28. 1st Line 1. All Transport will be accommodated in BOUZINCOURT AREA as troops move EAST of this Village. In the Event of orders being issued for evacuation of this village on account of shelling, etc -, Emergency Lines will be as follows :- 1. 97th Brigade) to "C" Emergency Line, with Pioneers) W.13.d.7.4. The above is marked by Boards on the ground.
Personnel.	29. Not more than 25 Officers will accompany the Battalion into action. Surplus Officers not detailed for duty by the Brigade will be accommodated in Huts at BOUZINCOURT with Town Major, and will proceed there on "X" day. Two senior N.C.O's or trained specialists will be left in Reserve, and will be accommodated in the Huts at BOUZINCOURT. The Town Major will arrange for the rationing of the party. Officers and N.C.O's proceeding to join their Units will take in addition to their Iron Ration, one day's Ration with them.
Arms and Equipment.	30. All Arms and Equipment of Wounded Men will accompany the wounded to the Field Ambulance.
Medical Arrangements	31. Medical Officer will be stationed on the night of Y/Z at Battalion Hqrs., junction of TOBERMORY and KILBERRY STREETS. Medical Officers will not move forward until the positions in front of them are taken by Troops. The Officer Commanding "B" Bearer-Sub-Division, 90th Field Ambulance will detail four Bearers to report on night of Y/Z to Medical Officer at Battalion Hqrs. Evacuation by THIEPVAL AVENUE (SOUTH) to HARLEY STREET and BLACK HORSE BRIDGE. Medical Officers must see that their dug-outs are protected with Blankets, and that Vermorel Sprayers and special solution are available. Medical Officers will arrange to carry forward their water-testing boxes, and examine wells at

7. O.O. No. 1

Medical Arrangements. 31. Contd.
THIEPVAL and MOUQUET FARME at the first opportunity.

Magazines. 32. Magazines for S.A.A. have been established at
Q.30.d.2.2., W.6.a.2.8., W.6.d.6.2.
Grenade Store at Battalion Hqrs., junction of TOBERMORY and KILBERRY STREETS.

Signal Communication. 33. The methods of communication for the offensive are as follows :-

(a) Telephone and Telegraph.
(b) Visual (Ground).
(c) Contact Aeroplanes.
(d) Wireless.
(e) Despatch Riders and Messengers.
(f) Pigeons.
(g) Visual (Balloons)

Brigade Signal Office will be established at point Q.36.d.9.0. (W.N. of Russian Sap. of SANDA STREET).

The above line will be extended to the enemy front line immediately that line is captured.

Messages will be handed in at this Office, thus saving the extra distance between the MAYFAIR front line and Brigade advanced Hqrs.

Battalion Signallers will take forward full establishment of Cable. Cables laid out during the advance, must be run outside the communication trenches. The onus of providing lateral communication lies with the Southern Unit.

Enemy's lines found in Hostile trenches should not be cut by Infantry ; they should be left to be dealt with by Signallers.

Should it be necessary to retire from the position that has been reached, any cables that have been run forward to it must be cut.

The contact Aeroplane will ascend at the commencement of the assult. It will be a B.E.2.c. and will have a black broad band under the right bottom plane. Communication will be made as follows :-

From Advanced Infantry. By flares or Roman Candles denoting 'We are here' and from flashing of mirrors.

Three flares or Roman Candles will be used fired in a row at three or four paces interval between each. ¼ minute between the firing of each flare.

From Battalion Headquarters.
By panneau (ground signalling sheet) or lamp.
The former will be used in preference to the latter whenever possible.

When wishing to signal, Brigades or Battalions will open ground sheet.

As soon as Aeroplane is in position to receive, ground station sends its unit call, meaning "H.Q." are here. this may be followed by one of the following signals :-

NN   meaning   "Short of Ammunition."
YY   ..   "Short of Grenades."
OO   ..   "Barrage required."
HH   ..   "Lengthen Range."
ZZ   ..   "Held up by Wire."
XX   ..   "Held up by Machine Gun Fire."

Each message will be repeated continuously in its entirety.

If necessary the signal may be followed by Map location of point or line, where barrage is wanted or range needed to be lengthened.

8. O.O. No. 1.

Signal Communication.   33. Contd.

No other signals will be used. Aeroplane will
acknowledge signals if possible, but will not
necessarily do so.
From Aeroplane.
White light meaning "Where are you".

Code Calls.

The ammended List of Code XXXXXX Calls issued under
G.91/5/7 will be used on all occasions during
operations.

W. D. Scott

Captain & Adjutant,
16th (Service) Battalion H.L.I.,

APPENDIX. 3.

16th (Service) Battalion H.L.I.

LIST OF CASUALTIES IN OFFICERS ON 1st JULY, 1916.

Killed in Action.

Captain D. B. Kerr,	A Coy.	
Lieut. T. Johnson.	D "	
2nd Lieut. R. S. Brown,	B "	
do. J. A. Brown,	B "	
do. J. A. Gemmill,	C "	
do. D. S. McHardy.	C "	

Missing, believed Killed.

2nd Lieut. J. Murdoch,	D Coy.	
do. J. Kerr,	A "	
do. G. McCurrach,	A "	

Wounded in Action :

Lieut. Col. & Hon. Col. D. Laidlaw.		
Major J. McElwain.	C Coy.	
Capt. & Adjt., W. D. Scott, (Still at Duty).		
Captain G. S. Fraser,	B Coy.	
Captain F. W. Reid,	D "	
2nd Lieut. R. A. Bogue,	A "	
do. R. Mitchell,	A "	
do. P. S. Hodgkinson,	B "	
do. J. Laing,	C "	
do. R. B. Stewart,	D "	
do. J. Cooper,	D "	

W. D. Scott

Captain & Adjutant,

16th (Servoce) Battalion H.L.I.,

31st July, 1916.

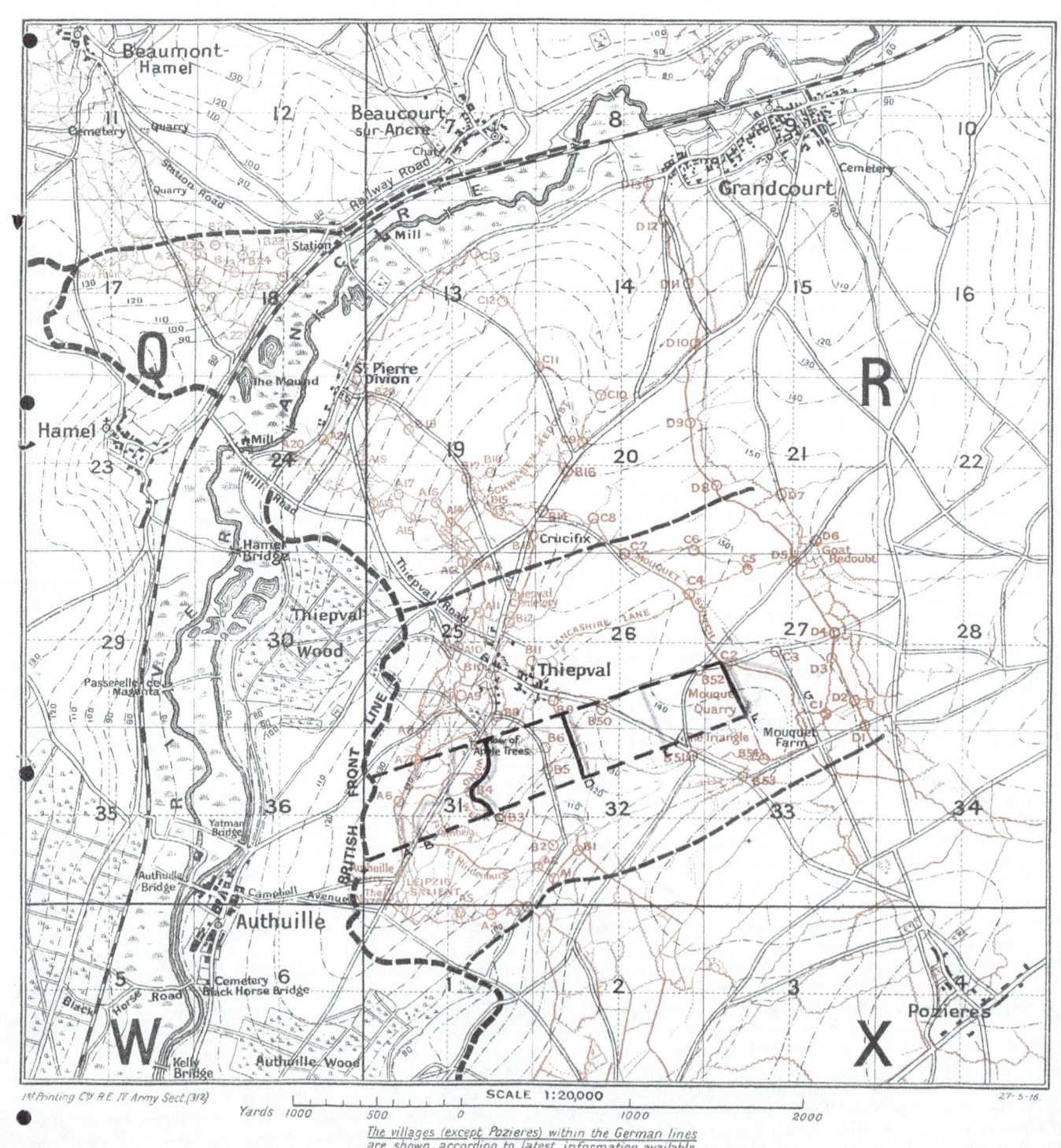

Confidential

vol 9

9.P.
7 sheets

War Diary
of the
16th (Service) Battalion Highland Light Infantry
Volume. 9.
From 1st till 31st August, 1916.

Army Form C. 2118.

Volume   *Page 1*

WAR DIARY
or
INTELLIGENCE SUMMARY.
(Erase heading not required.)

Instructions regarding War Diaries and Intelligence Summaries are contained in F.S. Regs., Part II. and the Staff Manual respectively. Title pages will be prepared in manuscript.

Hour, Date, Place	Summary of Events and Information	Remarks and references to Appendices
August, 1st BETHUNE	In Billets in BETHUNE	wet
2nd -do-	-do- -do-	wet
3rd -do-	-do- -do-	warm
4th -do-	-do- -do-	warm
5th -do-	-do- -do-	
	The Battalion moved from Billets in BETHUNE to CAMBRIN SECTOR, LEFT SUB-SECTOR and relieved the 2nd. Battalion Northamptonshire Regiment. Relief complete 5.30pm. Battalion on right 14th H.L.I. Battalion on Left 10th Dorset Regiment	wet
6th CAMBRIN SECTOR LEFT SUB-SECTOR	In occupancy of CAMBRIN LEFT SUB-SECTOR	wet

(73959) W4141—463. 400,000. 9/14. H.&J.Ltd. Forms/C. 2118/10.

Volume   Page 2.

Army Form C. 2118.

WAR DIARY
or
INTELLIGENCE SUMMARY.
(Erase heading not required.)

Instructions regarding War Diaries and Intelligence Summaries are contained in F.S. Regs., Part II. and the Staff Manual respectively. Title pages will be prepared in manuscript.

Hour, Date, Place	Summary of Events and Information	Remarks and references to Appendices
August 6th LEFT SUB-SECTOR	In occupancy of CAMBRIN LEFT SUB-SECTOR. The following Officers were posted to 16th H.L.I. 2nd Lieut J.S. Young from 4th H.L.I. " H. Duff " 13th H.L.I. " C.D. Mitchell " 4th H.L.I. " J. Gillies " 13th H.L.I. " M.E.C. Houston " 4th H.L.I.	W.D.J.
7th - do. -	In occupancy of CAMBRIN LEFT SUB-SECTOR 4 Other ranks wounded	W.D.J.
8th - do. -	In occupancy of CAMBRIN LEFT SUB-SECTOR 1 Other ranks killed Wounded 3 Other ranks	W.D.J.
9th - do. -	In occupancy of CAMBRIN LEFT SUB-SECTOR	W.D.J.
10th - do. -	In occupancy of CAMBRIN LEFT SUB-SECTOR 1 Other ranks wounded. The Battalion was relieved by 2nd K.O.Y.L.I. and moved to SUPPORT TRENCH, VILLAGE LINE. Relief complete 11. 30pm	W.D.J.

Volume   Page 3   Army Form C. 2118.

WAR DIARY
or
INTELLIGENCE SUMMARY.
(Erase heading not required.)

Instructions regarding War Diaries and Intelligence Summaries are contained in F. S. Regs., Part II. and the Staff Manual respectively. Title pages will be prepared in manuscript.

Hour, Date, Place	Summary of Events and Information	Remarks and references to Appendices
August 11th VILLAGE LINE CAMBRIN SECTOR	In SUPPORT CAMBRIN SECTOR (VILLAGE LINE)	W.D.J.
12th -do-	-do-	W.D.J.
13th -do-	-do-	W.D.J.
14th -do-	-do- Wounded 1 Other ranks. 2nd Lieutenant S.P. Jacoby transferred to 97th Trench Mortar Battery -do- Wounded 2 Other ranks	W.D.J.
	The Battalion relieved the 2nd K.O.Y.L.I. in CAMBRIN SECTOR, LEFT SUBSECTOR relief. 4:30pm complete. Battalion on right 17th H.L.I. Battalion on left 4th Dorset Regiment 15th H.L.I.	W.D.J.
15th CAMBRIN LEFT SUB-SECTOR	In occupation of CAMBRIN LEFT SUB-SECTOR Wounded 4 Other ranks	W.D.J.
16th -do- do	-do- Killed 3 Other ranks Wounded 4 Other ranks	W.D.J.

Army Form C. 2118.

Volume 9 Page 4

WAR DIARY
or
INTELLIGENCE SUMMARY.

(Erase heading not required.)

Instructions regarding War Diaries and Intelligence Summaries are contained in F. S. Regs., Part II. and the Staff Manual respectively. Title pages will be prepared in manuscript.

Hour, Date, Place	Summary of Events and Information	Remarks and references to Appendices
August, 17th CAMBRIN LEFT SUB-SECTOR	In occupation of CAMBRIN LEFT SUB-SECTOR. The Battalion was relieved by the 2nd K.O.Y.L.I. and proceeded to Billets in ANNEQUIN NORTH, as Battalion in Reserve. Relief complete 4:30 pm	W.O.S.
-do- 18th ANNEQUIN NORTH	In Billets ANNEQUIN NORTH	W.O.S.
-do- 19th -do-	-do-	W.O.S.
-do- 20th -do-	-do- Lieut H. Miller evacuated to England (sick) and Struck off Strength	W.O.S.
-do- 21st -do-	In Billets ANNEQUIN NORTH. The Battalion was relieved by the 11th Lancashires and proceeded to Billets in ANNEZIN	W.O.S.
-do- 22nd ANNEZIN	In Billets ANNEZIN	W.O.S.

Volume 9 Page 5

Army Form C. 2118.

Instructions regarding War Diaries and Intelligence Summaries are contained in F. S. Regs., Part II. and the Staff Manual respectively. Title pages will be prepared in manuscript.

WAR DIARY
or
INTELLIGENCE SUMMARY.
(Erase heading not required.)

Hour, Date, Place	Summary of Events and Information	Remarks and references to Appendices
August 23rd ANNEZIN	In Billets in ANNEZIN	wos.
—do— 24th MAZINGARBE	The Battalion left ANNEZIN at 7.30a.m., and proceeded to Huttments in MAZINGARBE. In Huttments MAZINGARBE	
	The Battalion relieved the 9th Battalion Royal Dublin Fusiliers in HULLUCH SECTION, RIGHT SUB-SECTION Relief complete 3p.m. Battalion on right 8th Royal Irish Fusiliers. Battalion on left 17th H.L.I.	wos.
—do— 25th HULLUCH RIGHT SUB-SECTION	In occupancy of HULLUCH RIGHT SUB-SECTION Battalion on night 6th Bedfordshire Regiment, on left 17th H.L.I.	wos.
—do— 26 —do—	In occupancy of HULLUCH RIGHT SUB-SECTION Wounded 1 Other ranks	wos.
—do— 27 —do—	—do— 2nd Lieut M.A. Hamilton Army Cyclist Corps, attached 16th R.I.S. attached for duty with 6th King's own Scottish Borderers	wos.
—do— 28 —do—	In HULLUCH RIGHT SUB-SECTION. The Battalion was relieved by 2nd K.O.Y.L.I., relief complete by 1p.m., and proceeded to TENTH AVENUE SUPPORT LINE (GERMAN SWITCH)	wos.
—do— 29 TENTH AVENUE HULLUCH SECTION	In Support TENTH AVENUE (GERMAN SWITCH)	wos.

Volume 9 Page 6

WAR DIARY
or
INTELLIGENCE SUMMARY.

Army Form C. 2118.

Hour, Date, Place	Summary of Events and Information	Remarks and references to Appendices
August 30th TENTH AVENUE HULLUCH SECTION	In Support TENTH AVENUE (GERMAN SWITCH)	w.p.S.
do - 3p.m. - do -	- do - The Battalion was relieved by the 1st Battalion Royal Scots Fusiliers and proceeded to Billets in BEUVRY. Relief complete 3pm.	w.p.S.

B. Hope Lieut. Colonel
Commanding 16th (Ser.) Bn. H.L.I.

97th Brigade.

32nd Division.

16th BATTALION

HIGHLAND LIGHT INFANTRY

SEPTEMBER 1 9 1 6

Confidential

To: D.A.G.,
　　　General Headquarters,
　　　　　3rd Echelon

Herewith, War Diary of the 16th (Service)
The Highland Light Infantry for the period 1st - 30th Sept., 1916.

Wm D. Scott
Major,
Commanding 16th High. L.I.

16TH BATTALION,
HIGHLAND LIGHT
INFANTRY.

No ....
Date ....

Vol 10

Confidential

War Diary

of the

16th (Service) Battalion The Highland Light Infantry

Volume 11.

From 1st - 30th September, 1916

Army Form C. 2118

WAR DIARY
or
INTELLIGENCE SUMMARY

of 16th (s) Bn. High.L.I.

(Erase heading not required.)

Instructions regarding War Diaries and Intelligence Summaries are contained in F. S. Regs., Part II. and the Staff Manual respectively. Title Pages will be prepared in manuscript.

Place	Date	Hour	Summary of Events and Information	Remarks and references to Appendices
BEUVRY	1st to 8th Sept.		In Billets in BEUVRY.	
BEUVRY	8th		The 16th High.L.I. relieved the 15th High.L.I. in CUINCHY SECTION (Right Sub-Section). Relief complete by 1 p.m. Battalion on right 16th North'd Fusrs., on left 17th High.L.I. 1 other rank wounded.	
CUINCHY SECTION.	9th		In CUINCHY SECTION (Right Sub-Section). The following Officers posted to this Battalion joined for duty on this date:- Lieut. N. H. McNeil, from 13th High.L.I. Lieut. A. Skene, from 13th High.L.I. 2nd Lieut. G. L. Davidson, from 4th High.L.I.	
CUINCHY SECTION.	10th		In CUINCHY SECTION (Right Sub-Section). Killed in Action - 1 other ranks.	
CUINCHY SECTION	11th		In CUINCHY SECTION (Right Sub-Section.)	
CUINCHY SECTION	12th		In CUINCHY SECTION (Right Sub-Section). Killed in Action - 1 other ranks. The following Officers posted to this Battalion joined for duty on this date:- 2nd Lieut. F. Scott, from 4th High.L.I. 2nd Lieut. F. W. Alexander, from 4th High.L.I. The Battalion was relieved by 2nd K.O.Y.L.I. in CUINCHY SECTION, and moved into Hutments in LE QUESNOY. Relief complete 5-30 p.m.	

Army Form C. 2118

WAR DIARY
or
INTELLIGENCE SUMMARY. 16th (S.) Bn. High.L.I.

(Erase heading not required.)

Instructions regarding War Diaries and Intelligence Summaries are contained in F. S. Regs., Part II. and the Staff Manual respectively. Title Pages will be prepared in manuscript.

Place	Date	Hour	Summary of Events and Information	Remarks and references to Appendices
LE QUESNOY	13th		In Hutments, LE QUESNOY.	nil.
LE QUESNOY	14th		In Hutments, LE QUESNOY. The undernoted Officer transferred to Royal Flying Corps is struck off from this date. Lieut. A. F. Wilson.	nil.
LE QUESNOY	15th		In Hutments, LE QUESNOY. The General Officer Commanding-in-Chief has under the authority of His Majesty The King, granted the undernoted awards :- DISTINGUISHED CONDUCT MEDAL. No. 14775 L/Sergeant John Anderson. MILITARY MEDAL. No. 14300 Pioneer Sergeant Colin Turner.	nil.
LE QUESNOY	16th		In Hutments, LE QUESNOY. The Battalion relieved the 2nd K.O.Y.L.I. in CUINCHY SECTION (Right Sub-Section). Relief complete, 4-30 p.m. Battalion on right : 16th North'd Fusrs., Battalion on left : 17th High.L.I.	nil.
CUINCHY SECTION.	17th		In CUINCHY SECTION (Right Sub-Section).	nil.
CUINCHY SECTION.	18th		In CUINCHY SECTION (Right Sub-Section). Killed in Action - 2 other ranks. Battalion on Right - 5/6th Bn. Royal Scots. Battalion on left 17th High.L.I.	nil.

1875 Wt. W593/826 1,000,000 4/15 J.B.C. & A. A.D.S.S./Forms/C. 2118.

WAR DIARY or INTELLIGENCE SUMMARY. High.L.I.

Army Form C. 2118

(Erase heading not required.)

Place	Date	Hour	Summary of Events and Information	Remarks and references to Appendices
CUINCHY SECTION.	19th		In CUINCHY SECTION (Right Sub-Section). 2 other ranks wounded. The undernoted Officer having been evacuated to England sick is struck off strength from this date - Captain W. McLaren.	roor
CUINCHY SECTION.	20th		In CUINCHY SECTION (Right Sub-Section). Killed in action - 2 other ranks ; Wounded : 2 other ranks. The Battalion was relieved by the 2nd K.O.Y.L.I., and proceed to VILLAGE LINE. as Battalion in Support. Relief complete - 4 p.m.	roor
CUINCHY SECTION	21st		In Support in VILLAGE LINE.	roor
CUINCHY SECTION	22nd.		In Support in VILLAGE LINE.	roor
CUINCHY SECTION	23rd		In Support in VILLAGE LINE.	roor
CUINCHY SECTION.	24th		In Support in VILLAGE LINE. 1 other ranks wounded. The Battalion relieved the 2nd K.O.Y.L.I. in CUINCHY Right Sub-Section. Relief complete - 4-30 p.m. Battalion on right - 15th High.L.I.; Battalion on left - 17th High.L.I. The General Officer Commanding-in-Chief, under authority granted by His Majesty the King, has made the undernoted award :- CROSS OF ST. GEORGE, 3rd CLASS. No. 14775 L/Sergeant John Anderson.	roor

WAR DIARY or INTELLIGENCE SUMMARY

16th Bn. High. L.I.

Army Form C. 2118

(Erase heading not required.)

Place	Date	Hour	Summary of Events and Information	Remarks and references to Appendices
CUINCHY SECTION	25th		In CUINCHY SECTION (Right Sub-Section) 4 other ranks wounded.	
CUINCHY SECTION	26th		In CUINCHY SECTION (Right Sub-Section.) The Battalion was relieved by the 2nd R. Innis Fusrs., and moved into Billets in BETHUNE. Relief complete by 12-30 p.m.	
BETHUNE	27th		In Billets, BETHUNE.	
BETHUNE	28th		In Billets, BETHUNE.	
BETHUNE	29th		In Billets, BETHUNE.	
BETHUNE	30th		In Billets, BETHUNE.	

Wm. D. Scott

Major,

Commanding 16th (Service) Battalion H.L.I.

97th Brigade.
32nd Division.

16th BATTALION

HIGHLAND LIGHT INFANTRY

OCTOBER 1 9 1 6

97/32

To :   D.A.G.,
            Base.

Herewith War Diary of the 16th
(Service) Battalion The Highland Light
Infantry from 1st to 31st October, 1916.

Wm D. Scott

            Major & Adjutant, for
    Lieut-Col. Cmdg. 16th High.L.I.

31st October, 1916.

Confidential

Vol 11

War Diary
of the
16th (Service) Battalion The Highland Light Infantry

Volume XI

1/31st October, 1916

Army Form C. 2118.

WAR DIARY
INTELLIGENCE SUMMARY
(Erase heading not required.)

Page 2.

Instructions regarding War Diaries and Intelligence Summaries are contained in F. S. Regs., Part II. and the Staff Manual respectively. Title Pages will be prepared in manuscript.

Place	Date	Hour	Summary of Events and Information	Remarks and references to Appendices
BETHUNE.	1st Oct.		In Billets BETHUNE.	any.
BETHUNE.	2nd		In Billets BETHUNE.	any.
BETHUNE.	3rd		In Billets BETHUNE.	any.
BETHUNE.	4th		In Billets BETHUNE. The Battalion relieved the 5/6th Royal Scots in Billets in ANNEQUIN. Relief complete 4 p.m.	any.
ANNEQUIN.	5th		In Billets, ANNEQUIN.	any.
ANNEQUIN.	6th		In Billets, ANNEQUIN.	any.
ANNEQUIN.	7th		In Billets, ANNEQUIN.	any.
ANNEQUIN.	8th		In Billets, ANNEQUIN. The Battalion relieved the 2nd K.O.Y.L.I. in the CAMBRIN Section, (left Sub-Section). Relief complete 4-20 p.m. Battalion on right 17th High.L.I., Battalion on left 16th North'd Fusrs.	any.
CAMBRIN Section.	9th		In CAMBRIN Left Sub-section.	any.
"	10th		In CAMBRIN left Sub-Section. Battalion on right 17th High.L.I., Battalion on left, 2nd K.O.Y.L.I. The undernoted Officers have joined the Battalion from to-day's date. 2nd Lieut. J. Halliday, 2nd Lieut. W.R. Bennie	any.
"	11th		In CAMBRIN Left Sub-section.	any.
"	12th		In CAMBRIN Left Sub-Section. 1 other ranks killed in Action. 1 Officer and 2 other ranks wounded.	any.
"	13th		In CAMBRIN Left Sub-section.	any.
"	14th		In CAMBRIN Left-Sub-Section. The Battalion was relieved by the 9th K.O.Y.L.I. and proceeded to Billets in BETHUNE. Relief complete 1 p.m.	any.

Page 2.

Army Form. C. 2118.

WAR DIARY
INTELLIGENCE SUMMARY

(Erase heading not required.)

Instructions regarding War Diaries and Intelligence Summaries are contained in F. S. Regs., Part II. and the Staff Manual respectively. Title Pages will be prepared in manuscript.

Place	Date	Hour	Summary of Events and Information	Remarks and references to Appendices
BETHUNE	15th Oct.		In Billets, BETHUNE. The Battalion marched from BETHUNE to Billets in MARLES MINES.	any.
MARLES MINES.	16th		In Billets MARLES MINES. The Battalion marched from MARLES MINES to Billets in OSTREVILLE.	any.
OSTREVILLE	17th		In Billets OSTREVILLE. The Battalion marched from OSTREVILLE to Billets in HOUVIN HOUVIGNEUL.	any.
HOUVIN HOUVIGNEUL	18th		In Billets HOUVIN HOUVIGNEUL. The Battalion marched from HOUVIN HOUVIGNEUL to Billets in LONGUEVILLETTE.	any.
LONGUEVILLETTE	19th		In Billets LONGUEVILLETTE.	any.
LONGUEVILLETTE	20th		In Billets LONGUEVILLETTE. The Battalion marched from LONGUEVILLETTE to Billets in RUBEMPRE.	any.
RUBEMPRE.	21st		In Billets RUBEMPRE.	any.
RUBEMPRE.	22nd		In Billets RUBEMPRE. The undernoted Officers having joined the Battalion are taken on strength from this date. 2nd Lieut. J. M. Bannatyne. 2nd Lieut. D. Dewar. 2nd Lieut. P. Crichton. 2nd Lieut. G. S. Hislop. 2nd Lieut. W. Beattie. The Battalion marched from RUBEMPRE to Billets in BOUZINCOURT.	any.
BOUZINCOURT.	23rd		In Billets BOUZINCOURT.	any.
BOUZINCOURT.	24th		In Billets BOUZINCOURT.	any.

2449 Wt. W14957/M90 750,000 1/16 J.B.C. & A. Forms/C.2118/12.

Page 3.

Army Form C. 2118.

WAR DIARY
INTELLIGENCE SUMMARY

(Erase heading not required.)

Instructions regarding War Diaries and Intelligence Summaries are contained in F. S. Regs., Part II. and the Staff Manual respectively. Title Pages will be prepared in manuscript.

Place	Date	Hour	Summary of Events and Information	Remarks and references to Appendices
BOUZINCOURT.	25th Oct.		In Billets, BOUZINCOURT.	any/.
BOUZINCOURT.	26th		In Billets, BOUZINCOURT.	any/.
BOUZINCOURT.	27th		In Billets, BOUZINCOURT.	any/.
BOUZINCOURT.	28th		In BILLETS, BOUZINCOURT.	any/.
BOUZINCOURT.	29th		In Billets, BOUZINCOURT. 2nd Lieut. J. S. Young wounded.	any/.
RUBEMPRE.	30th		In BILLETS, BOUZINCOURT. The Battalion marched from Billets in BOUZINCOURT to Billets in RUBEMPRE.	any/.
VAL DE MAISON.	31st		In Billets, RUBEMPRE. The Battalion marched from Billets in RUBEMPRE to encampment in LE VAL DE MAISON.	any/.

Lieut-Colonel,
Commanding 16th (Service) Battalion. H.L.I.

Confidential.

War Diary
of the
16th (Service) Battalion H.L.I.

Volume 13

From 1st to 30th November, 1916.

Volume 13 Page 1

16th H.L.I.

WAR DIARY
or
INTELLIGENCE SUMMARY

Army Form C. 2118.

Place	Date 1916 November	Hour	Summary of Events and Information	Remarks and references to Appendices
VAL-DE-MAISON	1-6th		Under Canvas in Encampment VAL-DE-MAISON	any
do	7th		Encampment VAL-DE-MAISON. The following Officer from 4th Bn. High. L.I. joined this Unit for duty on this date. 2nd Lieutenant J.W. Greig	any
do.	8-12th		Encampment VAL-DE-MAISON	any
do.	13th		Encampment VAL-DE-MAISON. The Battalion moved from Encampment VAL DE MAISON to Billets in HARPONVILLE	any
HARPONVILLE	14th		In Billets HARPONVILLE. The Battalion moved from Billets in HARPONVILLE to Hutments in PIONEER ROAD Near AVELUY	any
PIONEER ROAD	15th		In Hutments PIONEER ROAD. The Battalion moved from Hutments PIONEER ROAD to Billets in ENGLEBELMER. Draft of 15 O.R. joined unit this date.	any

WAR DIARY
or
INTELLIGENCE SUMMARY
(Erase heading not required.)

Volume 13 Page 2   16.4.A/9   Army Form C. 2118.

Instructions regarding War Diaries and Intelligence Summaries are contained in F. S. Regs., Part II. and the Staff Manual respectively. Title Pages will be prepared in manuscript.

Place	Date 1916 November	Hour	Summary of Events and Information	Remarks and references to Appendices
ENGLEBELMER	16		In Billets ENGLEBELMER. Verbal Orders were this day received by Commanding Officer that the Brigade would attack on morning of 18th MUNICH and FRANKFURT TRENCHES N.E. of [BEAUMONT HAMEL]	any
do	17		In Billets ENGLEBELMER	any
	17-19th		The Battalion under the Command of Lieut. Knife, marched to MAILLY-MAILLET and halted for a meal, and then proceeded to Brigade Headquarters at WHITE CITY. Guides were procured at this point, and the Battalion proceeded to assembly position at WAGON ROAD N.E. of BEAUMONT-HAMEL at 9.45p.m. The Guides lost their way and connection was broken between Companies, result being that when the assembly position was ultimately reached about 2 a.m., only "D" Company was intact. The other Coys latterly reached this point, but it was 6 a.m. before the whole Battalion was in Battle Position, which was as follows:- Right to left A-B-C-D- Companies with 17th H.L.I. on our right and 11th Border Regiment on our left. Zero time 6.10 a.m. Objectives (1) MUNICH TRENCH (2) FRANKFURT TRENCH	any

Volume 13. Page 3.

WAR DIARY
or
INTELLIGENCE SUMMARY

Army Form C. 2118.

16th H.L.I.

Place	Date	Hour	Summary of Events and Information	Remarks and references to Appendices
	1916 Nov. 14th		At Zero the Battalion moved forward and "D" Company and part of "C" Company succeeded in entering MUNICH TRENCH with little opposition. A Strong point with from 6 to 8 Machine Guns in the centre of S. Loop's front held up the other Coys and while part of the Battalion on our left also entered MUNICH TRENCH, the Battalion on our right was held up by Machine Gun fire. Three Platoons of "D" Company pushed forward and took FRANKFURT TRENCH, the remainder of the men having been left to mop up MUNICH TRENCH. Owing to the attack on our flanks having been unsuccessful, the enemy soon collected in large numbers, and lively bombing duels took place in MUNICH TRENCH. Our small party was quickly overwhelmed, and latterly every man a casualty. There was no support for the party which entered FRANKFURT TRENCH, but they hung on to the part that had captured, although isolated through the enemy being still in possession of his front line. The remnant of the Battalion took up position in WAGON ROAD in readiness for any Counter attack which might be launched. The Battalion was relieved by the 2nd Battalion Inniskilling Fusiliers on the morning of 19th November, 1916. Relief complete by 8.30 a.m.	

WAR DIARY

or

INTELLIGENCE SUMMARY

Volume 13 Page 4.

Army Form C. 2118.

Place	Date	Hour	Summary of Events and Information	Remarks and references to Appendices
November	1916 17.10th		The Battle Casualties were:— **Killed** Captain W.E. Johnson, 2nd Lieut G.M. Simpson, 2nd Lieut D.A. Milholm 2nd Lieut G.W. Campbell. 16 Other Ranks. **Wounded** Captain A. McPherson, 2nd Lieut H.A. Agnew, 2nd Lieut C.D. Mitchell 104 Other Ranks. **Missing** Lieut H. Skene, 2nd Lieut J. Stewart, 2nd Lieut J. Scott. 260 Other Ranks **Wounded and Missing** 2nd Lieut J.M. Bannatyne, 2nd Lieut W.M. Lyon, 2nd Lieut W. Duff. 10 Other Ranks. The Battalion on relief proceeded to Billets in MAILLY-MAILLET this date. 2nd Lieut W. McC. Murray from 1/4 H.L.I. joined Battalion on 18th November.	

Volume 13 Page 5

Army Form C. 2118.

WAR DIARY
or
INTELLIGENCE SUMMARY
(Erase heading not required.)

16th H.L.I.

Place	Date	Hour	Summary of Events and Information	Remarks and references to Appendices
MAILLY-MAILLET	1/16 November 20th		In Billets MAILLY- MAILLET 2nd Lieut. J. Workwashorn from 10th H.L.I. joined Battalion on this date	nil
do.		2/pt	In Billets MAILLY- MAILLET On the morning of this day 1 O.R. 11th Border Regiment reported to Brigade Headquarters at WHITE CITY that he was one of the party isolated in FRANKFURT TRENCH, and that he had succeeded during darkness in making his way through the enemy lines to our position. He stated that 3 Officers and 60 O.R. each of 11th Border Regiment and 16th H.L.I. were holding FRANKFURT TRENCH, and that the enemy seemed to be ignorant of their presence there. The G.O.C. decided that an attempt should be made that night to relieve the party, and orders were received from Brigade that the two Battalions concerned should each send 1 Officer and 30 O.R. to attempt a rescue. This party under command of Major Creighton proceeded to WAGON ROAD and thence took up a position 600 yards WEST of the MUNICH TRENCH opposite to that part of the Sector that our "D" Company had penetrated.	any

WAR DIARY or INTELLIGENCE SUMMARY

Volume 13 Page 6   Army Form C. 2118.

Place	Date	Hour	Summary of Events and Information	Remarks and references to Appendices
MAILLY-MAILLET	1916 Nov. 21st		Repeated efforts were made by patrols to get in touch with them, but the vigilance of the enemy in the MUNICH TRENCH prevented this.	nil
do	22nd		On the morning of 22nd Other two men of the party that was cut off and hiding out in FRANKFURT TRENCH, managed to get through the enemy's lines and reported that the isolated party would make any effort to break through sometime during the night. It was then arranged that a party of 1 Officer and 50 O.R. from each of the 16th High. L.I. and 11th Border Regiment would proceed and take up position 200 yards from the enemy line, so as to assist in case of the isolated party being attacked while attempting to break through. The party took up position about 8.30pm. and lay in wait until 6 am; but no attempt was made by the isolated party to break through.	nil

Volume 13 Page 7

16 th D.L.I.

WAR DIARY
or
INTELLIGENCE SUMMARY
(Erase heading not required.)

Army Form C. 2118.

Instructions regarding War Diaries and Intelligence Summaries are contained in F. S. Regs., Part II. and the Staff Manual respectively. Title Pages will be prepared in manuscript.

Place	Date 1916 November	Hour	Summary of Events and Information	Remarks and references to Appendices
MAILLY-MAILLET	23rd		In Billets MAILLY-MAILLET. The Battalion moved from MAILLY-MAILLET to Billets in RAINCHEVAL. Route: HEDAUVILLE — VARENNES — LEALVILLERS	any
RAINCHEVAL	24th		In Billets RAINCHEVAL	any
RAINCHEVAL	25th		In Billets RAINCHEVAL. The Battalion moved from RAINCHEVAL to Billets in GEZAINCOURT. Route: TERRAMESNIL — HULEUX.	any
GEZAINCOURT	26th		In Billets GEZAINCOURT. The Battalion proceeded from Billets in GEZAINCOURT to Billets in ST LEGER-L-DOMART	any
ST LEGER-L-DOMART	27th		In Billets ST LEGER-L-DOMART	any
do.	28th		In Billets ST LEGER-L-DOMART. The following Officer from 4th High L I joined for duty on this date 2nd Lieut A. C. B. Lennox.	any

Volume 13 Page 8

Army Form C. 2118.

WAR DIARY
or
INTELLIGENCE SUMMARY

(Erase heading not required.)

Instructions regarding War Diaries and Intelligence Summaries are contained in F. S. Regs., Part II. and the Staff Manual respectively. Title Pages will be prepared in manuscript.

16th H.L.I.

Place	Date	Hour	Summary of Events and Information	Remarks and references to Appendices
ST. LEGER-L-DOMART	November 1916 29		In Billets. 2nd Lieut Brotherspoon transferred to 15th H.L.I on this date. Authority NG 1364/120 G dated 23/11/16	
do.	30		do.	

R. Doyle Lieut Colonel,
Commanding 16th High L.I.

97th Brigade.
32nd Division.

16th BATTALION

HIGHLAND LIGHT INFANTRY

DECEMBER 1 9 1 6

13 P,
6 sheets

Vol 13

War Diary

of the

16th (Service) Battalion The Highland Light Infantry

Volume 7th
1st to 31st December, 1916

Volume 14. Page 1

WAR DIARY
or
INTELLIGENCE SUMMARY
(Erase heading not required.)

Army Form C. 2118

Place	Date 1916 December	Hour	Summary of Events and Information	Remarks and references to Appendices
ST LEGER-LES-DOMART.	1st		In Billets in ST LEGER-LES-DOMART. Draft of 40 Other Ranks joined Battalion on this date.	
Do.	2nd		In Billets in ST LEGER-LES-DOMART.	
Do.	3rd		In Billets in ST LEGER-LES-DOMART.	
Do.	4th		In Billets in ST LEGER-LES-DOMART.	
Do.	5th		In Billets in ST LEGER-LES-DOMART. The Battalion moved from ST LEGER-LES-DOMART to Billets in LANCHES, BARLETTE, HOUDAINCOURT.	
LANCHES, BARLETTE, HOUDAINCOURT	6th		In Billets in LANCHES, BARLETTE, HOUDAINCOURT. Lieut. H.A. Martin from 13th Highrs L.I., and draft of 33 Other Ranks joined Battalion for duty on this date.	

Volume 14 Page 2

Army Form C. 2118.

WAR DIARY
or
INTELLIGENCE SUMMARY
(Erase heading not required.)

Instructions regarding War Diaries and Intelligence Summaries are contained in F. S. Regs., Part II. and the Staff Manual respectively. Title Pages will be prepared in manuscript.

Place	Date	Hour	Summary of Events and Information	Remarks and references to Appendices
LANCHES, BARLETTE, HOUDAINCOURT	7th		In Billets in LANCHES, BARLETTE, HOUDAINCOURT	
Do.	8th		In Billets in LANCHES, BARLETTE, HOUDAINCOURT Draft of 33 Other Ranks taken on Strength on this date	
Do.	9th		In Billets in LANCHES, BARLETTE, HOUDAINCOURT Draft of 65 Other Ranks taken on Strength this date	
Do.	10th		In Billets in LANCHES, BARLETTE, HOUDAINCOURT	
Do.	11th		Do.	
Do.	12th		Do.	
Do.	13th		Do.	

Army Form C. 2118.

WAR DIARY
or
INTELLIGENCE SUMMARY
(Erase heading not required.)

Volume 14 Page 3

Instructions regarding War Diaries and Intelligence Summaries are contained in F.S. Regs., Part II. and the Staff Manual respectively. Title Pages will be prepared in manuscript.

Place	Date 1916 December	Hour	Summary of Events and Information	Remarks and references to Appendices
LANCHES, BARLETTE, HOUDAINCOURT	14th		In Billets LANCHES, BARLETTE, HOUDAINCOURT Draft of 91 Other Ranks taken on Strength this date	
Do.	15th		In Billets LANCHES, BARLETTE, HOUDAINCOURT	
Do.	16th		Do. Do. The following Officers joined Battalion for duty on this date Captain L. Garbside 1st High. L.I. from 50th Infantry Brigade 2nd Lieut. H. H. Taylor from 19th High. L.I. 2nd Lieut. A.G. Clark from 3rd High. L.I. 2nd Lieut. J.L. Frew from 13th High. L.I. The Battalion moved from Billets in LANCHES to Billets in BERTEAUCOURT.	
BERTEAUCOURT	17th		In Billets BERTEAUCOURT The Battalion moved from Billets in BERTEAUCOURT to Billets in RUBEMPRÉ	
	18th		In Billets RUBEMPRÉ Draft of 6 Other Ranks taken on Strength on this date.	
	19th		In Billets RUBEMPRÉ	

WAR DIARY
or
INTELLIGENCE SUMMARY

(Erase heading not required.)

Volume 14 Page 4

Place	Date	Hour	Summary of Events and Information	Remarks and references to Appendices
RUBEMPRÉ	1916 December 20th		In Billets RUBEMPRÉ	
Do.	21st		Draft of 13 Other Ranks taken on Strength this date	
Do	22nd		In Billets RUBEMPRÉ	
Do	23rd		In Billets RUBEMPRÉ	
Do.	24th		In Billets RUBEMPRÉ	
Do.	25th		In Billets RUBEMPRÉ	
			Draft of 7 Other Ranks taken on Strength this date.	
Do	26th		In Billets RUBEMPRÉ	
Do	27th		In Billets RUBEMPRÉ	
Do	28th		In Billets RUBEMPRÉ	

WAR DIARY
or
INTELLIGENCE SUMMARY

(Erase heading not required.)

Army Form C. 2118

Volume 14 Page 5

Place	Date	Hour	Summary of Events and Information	Remarks and references to Appendices
RUBEMPRÉ	December 1916 29th		In Billets RUBEMPRÉ The following Officers joined the Battalion for duty on this date:— 2nd Lieut. A.C. Anderson from G.H.Q. Cadet School. 2nd Lieut. G.C. Dixon from 4th High. L.I.	
Do.	30th		In Billets RUBEMPRÉ	
Do.	31st		In Billets RUBEMPRÉ	

Wm. D. Scott
Major,
Commanding 16th High. L.I.

Confidential

War Diary

of the

16th (Service) Battalion Sigh. L.I.

Volume 15

1st to 31st January, 1917.

Vol 14

WAR DIARY or INTELLIGENCE SUMMARY

Army Form C. 2118

Volume 15 Page 1

Instructions regarding War Diaries and Intelligence Summaries are contained in F. S. Regs., Part II. and the Staff Manual respectively. Title Pages will be prepared in manuscript.

(Erase heading not required.)

Place	Date 1917 January	Hour	Summary of Events and Information	Remarks and references to Appendices
RUBEMPRÉ	1st		In Billets RUBEMPRÉ	nil
RUBEMPRÉ	2nd		In Billets RUBEMPRÉ	nil
RUBEMPRÉ	3rd		In Billets RUBEMPRÉ	nil
RUBEMPRÉ	4th		In Billets RUBEMPRÉ	nil
RUBEMPRÉ	5th		In Billets RUBEMPRÉ	nil
RUBEMPRÉ	6th		In Billets RUBEMPRÉ. The Battalion moved Billets in RUBEMPRÉ to Hutments in COURCELLES-AU-BOIS	nil
COURCELLES	7th		The Battalion moved from Hutments in COURCELLES to SERRE LEFT SUB-SECTOR and relieved the 8th Bn King's Own Royal Lancs. Regt. Relief complete 10.35pm	nil
SERRE LEFT SUB-SECTOR	8th		In occupation of SERRE LEFT SUB-SECTOR	nil
SERRE LEFT SUB-SECTOR	9th		In occupation of SERRE LEFT SUB-SECTOR. The following Officers joined Battalion for duty:- 2nd Lieut J. McClellan 2nd Lieut A.F. Ferguson Major A. Fraser 2nd Lieut J. Somerville 2nd Lieut W. Rodger 2nd Lieut C.B. Grant 2nd Lieut J. Middlemas	nil

WAR DIARY or INTELLIGENCE SUMMARY

(Erase heading not required.)

Army Form C. 2118.

Volume 15 Page 2

Place	Date 1917 January	Hour	Summary of Events and Information	Remarks and references to Appendices
SERRE LEFT SUB-SECTOR	10th		In occupation of SERRE LEFT SUB-SECTOR. The Battalion was relieved by the 2nd K.O.Y.L.I. and moved to Billets in COURCELLES. Relief complete 10.50pm.	nil
COURCELLES	11th		In Hutments COURCELLES	nil
COURCELLES	12th		In Hutments COURCELLES. The Battalion relieved the 2nd K.O.Y.L.I., in SERRE SUB-SECTOR Relief complete 11.15pm	nil
SERRE LEFT SUB-SECTOR	13th		In SERRE LEFT SUB-SECTOR. 1 or. Wounds 6 or. Missing	nil
SERRE LEFT SUB-SECTOR	14th		In SERRE LEFT SUB-SECTOR. The Battalion was relieved by the 16th Northumberland Fusiliers and moved into Hutments at BUS. Relief complete 2 am. The following Officer joined the Battalion for duty on this date 2nd Lieut. @.C.M.Petram	nil
BUS	15th		In Hutments BUS	nil
BUS	16th		In Hutments BUS	nil
BUS	17th		In Hutments BUS	nil

WAR DIARY or INTELLIGENCE SUMMARY

Army Form C. 2118

Volume 15 Page 3

Place	Date 1917 January	Hour	Summary of Events and Information	Remarks and references to Appendices
BUS	18th		In Hutments BUS	nil
BUS	19th		In Hutments BUS	nil
BUS	20th		In Hutments BUS	nil
			The Battalion moved from Hutments BUS to SUPPORT LINE BEAUMONT HAMEL	
BEAUMONT HAMEL	21st		In Support BEAUMONT HAMEL	nil
BEAUMONT HAMEL	22nd		In Support BEAUMONT HAMEL	nil
BEAUMONT HAMEL	23rd		In Support BEAUMONT HAMEL. The Battalion relieved 1 Coy 11th Border Regt, and 3 Coys of 2nd K.O.Y.L.I, on R.2. Sub-sector. Relief complete by 12.15 a.m.	nil
R.2. SUB-SECTOR	24th		In occupation of R.2. Sub-sector	nil
R.2. SUB-SECTOR	25th		In occupation of R.2. Sub-sector. The Battalion was relieved by the 2nd K.O.Y.L.I., and moved to Support Line BEAUMONT HAMEL. Relief complete 10.30 pm	nil

Army Form C. 2118

Volume 15 Page 4

WAR DIARY
or
INTELLIGENCE SUMMARY
(Erase heading not required.)

Instructions regarding War Diaries and Intelligence Summaries are contained in F. S. Regs., Part II. and the Staff Manual respectively. Title Pages will be prepared in manuscript.

Place	Date 1917 January	Hour	Summary of Events and Information	Remarks and references to Appendices
BEAUMONT HAMEL	26th		In Support BEAUMONT HAMEL	nil
BEAUMONT HAMEL	27th		In Support BEAUMONT HAMEL. The Battalion relieved the 17th H.L.I. in R.1. Subsector. Relief complete 6.45pm	nil
R.1. SUB-SECTOR	28th		In occupation of R.1. Subsector	nil
R.1. SUB-SECTOR	29th		In occupation of R.1. Subsector	nil
R.1. SUB-SECTOR	30th		In occupation of R.1. Subsector	nil
R.1. SUB-SECTOR	31/01		In occupation of R.1. Subsector. The Battalion moved from R.1. Subsector, on being relieved by 11th Border Regt, and proceeded to Support Line BEAUMONT HAMEL. Relief complete 9.45pm. 1 O.R. killed 5 O.R. wounded	nil

John Hunter Captain, ?/High L.I.
Commanding 16th High L.I.

To: Headquarters,
    97th Inf Bde.

Herewith War Diary of this Battalion for the month of February, 1917.

Andw. Macfarlane
Lieut & Adjt., for
Lt Col., Commanding 16th H.L.I.

16TH BATTALION,
HIGHLAND LIGHT
INFANTRY.
No. OR.16/112
Date 28-2-17

28/2/17

Confidential

Vol 15

15.P.
6 sheets

War Diary.

of the

16th (Service) Bn Highland Light Infantry

Volume 16

From 1st to 28th February, 1917

Army Form C. 2118

VOLUME 16 PAGE 1.

WAR DIARY
or
INTELLIGENCE SUMMARY
(Erase heading not required.)

Instructions regarding War Diaries and Intelligence Summaries are contained in F. S. Regs., Part II. and the Staff Manual respectively. Title Pages will be prepared in manuscript.

Place	Date 1917 FEBY.	Hour	Summary of Events and Information	Remarks and references to Appendices
BEAUMONT HAMEL.	1st		In Brigade Reserve in BEAUMONT HAMEL. 1 Other Rank wounded.	any.
BEAUMONT HAMEL	2nd		In Brigade Reserve in BEAUMONT HAMEL. The Battalion relieved the 2nd K.O.Y.L.I., in R.2. Subsector. Relief complete 10.45 p.m. 1 O.R. wounded.	any.
R.2. Subsector	3rd		In occupation of R.2. Subsector.	any.
R.2. Subsector	4th		In occupation of R.2. Subsector.	any.
R.2. Subsector	5th		In occupation of R.2. Subsector. 2 Other Ranks wounded.	any.
R.2. Subsector	6th		In occupation of R.2. Subsector	any.
R.2. Subsector	7th		In occupation of R.2. Subsector. The Battalion was relieved by the 17th H.L.I., and proceeded to Brigade Reserve in BEAUMONT HAMEL. Relief complete 8.30 p.m. 1 Other Rank wounded.	any.
BEAUMONT HAMEL	8th		In Brigade Reserve in BEAUMONT HAMEL 1 Other Rank wounded.	any.
BEAUMONT HAMEL	9th		In Brigade Reserve in BEAUMONT HAMEL 2 Other Ranks wounded.	any.

WAR DIARY or INTELLIGENCE SUMMARY

VOLUME 16 PAGE 2

Army Form C. 2118

Place	Date	Hour	Summary of Events and Information	Remarks and references to Appendices
BEAUMONT HAMEL	10th		In Brigade Reserve in BEAUMONT HAMEL.	nil
BEAUMONT HAMEL	11th		In Brigade Reserve in BEAUMONT HAMEL. 3 Other Ranks wounded.	nil
BEAUMONT HAMEL	12th		In Brigade Reserve in BEAUMONT HAMEL. The Battalion relieved the 11th Border Regt. and 1 Coy of the 16th Lancashire Fusiliers in R.1. Subsector. Relief complete 5.30 a.m.	nil
R.1. Subsector	13th		In occupation of R.1. Subsector 12 Other Ranks wounded.	nil
R.1. Subsector	14th		In occupation of R.1. Subsector. The Battalion was relieved by the 2/5th West Yorks. and marched to hutments at OLDHAM CAMP, MAILLY-MAILLET. Relief complete 1.50 a.m. 15th February. 3 Other Ranks wounded.	nil
OLDHAM CAMP	15th		In hutments in OLDHAM CAMP	nil
OLDHAM CAMP	16th		In hutments OLDHAM CAMP.	nil
OLDHAM CAMP	17th		In hutments OLDHAM CAMP. The Battalion moved by bus from OLDHAM CAMP to Billets in PIERREGOT.	nil
PIERREGOT	18th		In Billets PIERREGOT. The following Officers joined the Battalion on this date :- Capt A.W. McCallum from 78th T.R. Battalion. Lieut W.E. Garret-Fisher from 78th T.R. Battalion.	nil

Army Form C. 2118

WAR DIARY
or
INTELLIGENCE SUMMARY

(Erase heading not required.)

VOLUME 16 PAGE 3.

Instructions regarding War Diaries and Intelligence Summaries are contained in F.S. Regs., Part II. and the Staff Manual respectively. Title Pages will be prepared in manuscript.

Place	Date 1917 FEBY	Hour	Summary of Events and Information	Remarks and references to Appendices
PIERREGOT	19th		In Billets in PIERREGOT.	nil
PIERREGOT	20th		In Billets in PIERREGOT.	nil
PIERREGOT	21st		In Billets in PIERREGOT. The Battalion moved from Billets in PIERREGOT to Billets in RIVERY.	nil
RIVERY	22nd		In Billets in RIVERY. The Battalion moved from Billets in RIVERY to Billets in MARCELCAVE.	nil
MARCELCAVE	23rd		In Billets in MARCELCAVE	nil
MARCELCAVE	24th		In Billets in MARCELCAVE	nil
MARCELCAVE	25th		In Billets in MARCELCAVE. The Battalion moved from Billets in MARCELCAVE to Billets in MEZIERES.	nil
MEZIERES.	26th		In Billets in MEZIERES.	nil
MEZIERES.	27th		In Billets in MEZIERES. The Battalion moved from Billets in MEZIERES to Billets in BEAUFORT	nil
BEAUFORT	28th		In Billets in BEAUFORT.	nil

Lieut Colonel,
Commanding, 16th (Service) Battalion H.L.I.

To : Headquarters,
   97th Infantry Brigade.

Herewith War Diary for March, 1917.

Andw. Macfarlane
        Lieut & Adjt., for
Lieut Col., Commanding, 16th High. L. I.

31st March, 1917.

To : D.A.G.,
   General Headquarters,
      3rd Echelon.

   ---------- -

Herewith War Diary of the 16th Battalion Highland Light Infantry for the period 1st to 31st March, 1917.

Andro Macfarlane

Lieut & Adjutant, for
Lieut Col., Commanding, 16th High. L. I.

31st March, 1917.

Vol/6

16.P.
6 sheets

CONFIDENTIAL

WAR DIARY

OF THE

16TH(SERVICE) BATTALION HIGHLAND LIGHT INFANTRY

VOLUME 17

1st to 31st March, 1917.

Volume 17 Page 1

Army Form C. 2118.

WAR DIARY
or
INTELLIGENCE SUMMARY.
(Erase heading not required.)

Instructions regarding War Diaries and Intelligence Summaries are contained in F. S. Regs., Part II. and the Staff Manual respectively. Title pages will be prepared in manuscript.

Place	Date 1917 March	Hour	Summary of Events and Information	Remarks and references to Appendices
BEAUFORT	1st		In Billets BEAUFORT	
BEAUFORT	2nd		In Billets BEAUFORT The Battalion relieved the 15th Lancashire Fusiliers in the Left Subsector, Left Sector relief complete 12.50 a.m. 3rd March, 1917.	
Left SUB-Sector	3rd		In occupation of the Left SUB-SECTOR, FOUQUESCOURT Casualties Killed 2 Other Ranks Wounded 3 Other Ranks	
LEFT SUB-SECTOR	4th		In occupation of the Left SUB-SECTOR, FOUQUESCOURT	
LEFT SUB-SECTOR	5th		In occupation of the Left SUB-SECTOR. The Battalion was relieved by the 2nd K.O.Y.L.I., and proceeded to Brigade Reserve in WARVILLERS. Relief complete 11.10p.m.	
WARVILLERS	6th		In occupation of WARVILLERS (Brigade Reserve)	
WARVILLERS	7th		In Brigade Reserve WARVILLERS	
WARVILLERS	8th		In Brigade Reserve WARVILLERS The Battalion relieved the 2nd K.O.Y.L.I. in the Left SUB-SECTION. Relief complete 8.50 p.m.	
LEFT SUB-SECTION	9th		In occupation of the LEFT SUB-SECTION, FOUQUESCOURT	
LEFT SUB-SECTION	10th		In occupation of the LEFT SUB-SECTION The Battalion was relieved by the 18th Lancashire Fusiliers, and proceeded to Billets in WARVILLERS. relief complete 8.40 p.m.	
WARVILLERS	11th		In Brigade Reserve WARVILLERS	

Volume 17 Page 2.   Army Form C. 2118.

WAR DIARY
or
INTELLIGENCE SUMMARY.

(Erase heading not required.)

Place	Date 1917.	Hour	Summary of Events and Information	Remarks and references to Appendices
	March			
WARVILLERS	12th		In Brigade Reserve WARVILLERS.	nil
WARVILLERS	13th		In Brigade Reserve WARVILLERS.	nil
WARVILLERS	14th		In Brigade Reserve WARVILLERS. The Battalion was relieved by the 5/6th Royal Scots, and proceeded to Billets in FRESNOY-EN-CHAUSSEE. Relief complete 8.30 p.m.	nil
FRESNOY EN CHAUSSEE	15th		In Billets in FRESNOY-EN-CHAUSSEE	nil
FRESNOY EN CHAUSSEE	16th		In Billets in FRESNOY-EN-CHAUSSEE.	nil
FRESNOY-EN CHAUSSEE	17th		In Billets in FRESNOY-EN-CHAUSSEE The Battalion proceeded to LE QUESNOY	nil
LE QUESNOY	18th		In Dug Outs LE QUESNOY The Battalion proceeded to FRESNOY-LES-ROYE	nil
FRESNOY-LES ROYE	19th		In Billets FRESNOY-LES-ROYE The Battalion moved from FRESNOY to ETALON arriving there at 1.30p.m. The Battalion moved from ETALON to NESLE	nil
NESLE	20th		In Billets in NESLE	nil
NESLE	21st		In Billets in NESLE	nil

Volume 17 Page 2.

Army Form C. 2118.

WAR DIARY
or
INTELLIGENCE SUMMARY.
(Erase heading not required.)

Instructions regarding War Diaries and Intelligence Summaries are contained in F. S. Regs. Part II. and the Staff Manual respectively. Title pages will be prepared in manuscript.

Place	Date 1917. March	Hour	Summary of Events and Information	Remarks and references to Appendices
NESLE	22nd		In Billets in NESLE	any
NESLE	23rd		In Billets in NESLE	any
NESLE	24th		In Billets in NESLE	any
NESLE	25th		In Billets in NESLE	any
NESLE	26th		In Billets in NESLE 2nd Lieut M.I.McInnes from 6th (R) Bn H.L.I. joined Battalion for duty on this date	any
NESLE	27th		In Billets in NESLE The Battalion moved from Billets in NESLE to Billets in FERME DE MONTIELLE	any
FERME DE MONTIELLE	28th		In Billets in FERME DE MONTIELLE The Battalion moved from Billets in FERME DE MONTIELLE and relieved Cavalry OUTPOSTS at VAUX, ETREILLERS, and CHATEAU DE POMMERY	any
VAUX ETREILLERS Ch DE POMMERY	29th		Holding OUTPOSTS at VAUX, ETREILLERS and CHATEAU DE POMMERY. 2nd Manchester Regiment on left (22nd Division(French) on right. Casualties 2 Killed 8 o.r. Wounded	any
-DO-	30th		Holding OUTPOSTS at VAUX, ETREILLERS, and CHATEAU DE POMMERY Casualties 1 o.r Killed 4 o.r. Wounded	any
-DO-	31st		Holding OUTPOSTS at VAUX, ETREILLERS, and CHATEAU DE POMMERY.	any

Lieut Colonel,
Commanding, 16th (Service) Battalion, Highland Light Infantry

16th (Service) Bn High L.I.

Honours and Awards

Distinguished Service Order

Captain Andrew McPherson   18/11/16

Military Cross

Captain	William McLaren	1/7/16
Lieut	Robert A. Bogue	1/7/16
Major	Wm D. Scott	1/1/17
Lieut	H.A. Martin	10/2/17
Captain	V.E. Badcock (R.A.M.C)	3/4/17

Distinguished Conduct Medal

14775   A/Sgt   J. Anderson   1/7/16

Military Medal

14196	Sgt	D. Kennedy	4/6/16
15119	Pte	J. Cranford	4/6/16
3359	Pte	J. Shepherd	4/6/16
15066	Sgt	W. McCombe	4/6/16
14130	L/C.	J. Cumbuland	4/6/16
14300	Sgt	C. Turner	1/7/16
15037	Sgt	E. McFarlane	1/7/16
14365	Sgt	S. Kelso	1/7/16
15130	Sgt	R. Turner	18/11/16
14325	Sgt	J. Johnston	18/11/16
14362	Sgt	J. Mack	18/11/16
14492	Pte	W. Thomson	18/11/16
31610	Pte	S. McKay	18/11/16
43101	Pte	G. Wallace	14/3/17
14853	Pte	J. Finlayson	14/3/17
10396	Sgt	A. Terrington	14/3/17
14267	Pte	G. Ross	14/3/17
14315	Cpl	R. Wylie	3/4/17
12095	A/Cpl	J. Richardson	3/4/17
30530	Pte	J. Low	14/4/17
7063	Sgt	J. Brown	14/4/17
14677	L/Sgt	A.K. Fleck	19/3/17
14948	Pte	J. Rodgers	19/3/17
3540	Pte	J. Shankland	19/3/17

Bar to Military Medal

14365   Sgt   S. Kelso   14/3/17

Mention in Despatches

Lt Colonel	D. Laidlaw, V.D.	30/4/17
15066 Sergt	W. McCombe	30/4/17
Lieut & Q.M.	R. Simpson	25/5/17
Captain	A. McPherson	25/5/17
Captain	T.E. Badcock (RAMC)	29/5/17
R.S.M.	G.J. Taylor	25/5/17

Russian Cross of St. George (3rd Class)

14775 L/Sgt. J. Anderson — 1/7/16

Medaille Militaire

30530 Pte J. Low — 14/4/17

To: Headquarters,
    97th Inf. Bde.

Herewith War Diary for the month
of April. 1917

R. Fyfe Lieut Colonel,
Comdg. 16th H.L.I.

304/7.

Army Form C. 2118.

WAR DIARY
or
INTELLIGENCE SUMMARY

(Erase heading not required.)

Volume 18 page 1.

Instructions regarding War Diaries and Intelligence Summaries are contained in F.S. Regs., Part II. and the Staff Manual respectively. Title Pages will be prepared in manuscript.

Place	Date 1917 April	Hour	Summary of Events and Information	Remarks and references to Appendices
ETREILLERS	1st		In occupation of Outpost Line in front of ETREILLERS. Battalion Headquarters in VAUX. The Battalion was relieved by the 18th Battalion Lancashire Fusiliers and withdrew to Bivouac in VAUX, relief being complete by 11.15 p.m.	
VAUX	2nd		In Bivouac VAUX. The Battalion was ordered to take up a position in front of ROUPY to fill a gap 1,800 yards between the 96th Infantry Brigade on the left and the French on the right. Our right flank to rest on the ROUPY – ST QUENTIN ROAD. The Battalion left VAUX at 11 a.m. and proceeded to take up above position. The dispositions from Right to Left were D, C, A, Companies with B Company in support in QUARRY point F.12.a.1.1. Battalion Headquarters were established in the QUARRY. The line was reached about 2 p.m., and Companies proceeded to dig in. Although the enemy opened machine gun fire and shelled the position our casualties were only 1 Other Rank Killed and 5 Other Ranks wounded, and by dusk a continuous traversed trench had been dug. Between 5 and 10 p.m. an almost continuous bombardment of the QUARRY was carried out by the enemy, and our casualties were very heavy. Casualties Killed in Action Captain A.M. McCallum and 1 Other Rank Wounded in Action Captain V.E. Badcock R.A.M.C. Captain (Act Major) J. Hunter 2/Lieut J. Robertson 26 Other Ranks Draft of 25 Other Ranks joined Unit on this date.	
ROUPY VAUX	3rd		In occupation of Outpost line at ROUPY. Draft of 52 Other Ranks joined Unit on this date.	

2449 Wt. W14957/M90 750,000 1/16 J.B.C. & A. Forms/C.2118/12.

VOLUME 18 Page 2.

Army Form C. 2118.

WAR DIARY
or
INTELLIGENCE SUMMARY

(Erase heading not required.)

Instructions regarding War Diaries and Intelligence Summaries are contained in F. S. Regs., Part II. and the Staff Manual respectively. Title Pages will be prepared in manuscript.

Place	Date 1917 April	Hour	Summary of Events and Information	Remarks and references to Appendices
ROUPY	4th		In occupation of Outpost line in front of ROUPY. At 3.30 p.m. the French on our Right attacked EPINE DE DALLON, their left flank crossing our front and joining with Right Flank of 96th Infantry Brigade.	
ROUPY	5th		In Outpost line in front of ROUPY. The Battalion withdrew to ATTILLY.	
ATTILLY	6th		In Brigade Reserve ATTILLY.	
ATTILLY	7th		In Brigade Reserve ATTILLY. Major Wm D Scott, M.C., rejoined Unit from Senior Officers' Course ALDERSHOT on this date. 2nd Lieut G.G. Lean from 9th High. L. I., joined Battalion for duty on this date.	
ATTILLY	8th		In Brigade Reserve ATTILLY.	
ATTILLY	9th		In Brigade Reserve ATTILLY Casualties Killed in Action 1 Other Rank Wounded in Action 4 Other Ranks Draft of 48 Other Ranks joined Battalion on this date.	
ATTILLY	10th		In Brigade Reserve ATTILLY	
ATTILLY	11th		In Brigade Reserve ATTILLY	
ATTILLY	12th		In Brigade Reserve ATTILLY Draft of 5 Other Ranks joined Battalion on this date.	
ATTILLY	13th		In Brigade Reserve ATTILLY.	

Volume 18 Page 3.

Army Form C. 2118.

Instructions regarding War Diaries and Intelligence Summaries are contained in F. S. Regs., Part II. and the Staff Manual respectively. Title Pages will be prepared in manuscript.

WAR DIARY
or
INTELLIGENCE SUMMARY
(Erase heading not required.)

Place	Date	Hour	Summary of Events and Information	Remarks and references to Appendices
ATTILLY	14th		The Battalion left ATTILLY at 1.30 a.m. to take up Battle position in front of SELENCY for an attack on FAYET at 4.30 a.m. The assembly position was from S.4.c.5.1. to S.4.a.2.1. "B" & "A" Coys formed the First two waves, and "D" & "C" Coys formed the second two waves "D" Coy being on the Right. Battalion Headquarters were at point S.3.d.8.3. The 2nd K.O.Y.L.I., were on our left. The First Objective was a N. & S. line through FAYET CHATEAU to be captured by "B" & "A" Coys. The 2nd Objective the GRICOURT - ST QUENTIN ROAD to be captured by "D" & "C" Coys, a Defensive Flank being formed by "B" & "A" Coys to the right after "D" & "C" Coys had passed through their line. The attack was launched at 4.30 a.m., the artillery making a magnificent barrage, and the men keeping close up to this got on well. The enemy seemed to be taken by surprise and showed little fight, the result being that many prisoners were taken. The 1st Objective was reached about 50 minutes after zero. The whole of FAYET two a mass of ruins and some difficulty was experienced in maintaining direction, the result being that "D" & "C" Coys got too far right and took up a line on the road running through S.6.c. and S.12.a. This line was held. The Brigade phoned to say that a Battalion of 14th Infantry Brigade were attacking CEPY FARM at 3.30 p.m., and our final Objective was to be captured at same time. Before this message was received, however "D" & "C" Coys had launched an attack and the final Objective was gained at 2 p.m. with few casualties. In conjunction with 2nd Manchester Regiment on the Right the hostile trench running across our front from CEPY FARM was taken at 4 p.m. Our dispositions now were "C" & "D" Coys in front line with "A" & "B" Coys in support in front of wood at S.6.a. At 5 p.m. we were ordered to extend our front as far as CEPY FARM exclusive and "B" Coy relieved 1 Coy of 2nd Manchester Regiment at 7 p.m. "A" Coy then moved forward to sunken road and were in immediate support. Considering that all our objectives were gained our casualties were not heavy and the Battalion captured 2 Machine Guns and about 150 prisoners. The telegrams of congratulation received are shown in appendix 1. Operation Orders are attached as appendix 2.	

VOLUME 18 page 4.

WAR DIARY
or
INTELLIGENCE SUMMARY

(Erase heading not required.)

Army Form C. 2118.

Instructions regarding War Diaries and Intelligence Summaries are contained in F. S. Regs, Part II. and the Staff Manual respectively. Title Pages will be prepared in manuscript.

Place	Date 1917 April	Hour	Summary of Events and Information	Remarks and references to Appendices

	14th		The casualties were as follows :-
			
			         Killed in Action
			
			    Lieut (Act. Capt) J.S. Wilkie
			    2nd Lieut F.W. Alexander
			    13 Other ranks
			
			         Wounded in Action
			
			    2nd Lieut A.J. Sanders
			    2nd Lieut J.L. Frew
			    2nd Lieut W. Rodger
			    2nd Lieut A.C. Anderson
			    96 Other ranks	

GRICOURT - St QUENTIN ROAD	15th		In occupation of line in front of GRICOURT - ST QUENTIN ROAD, Fayet was heavily shelled intermittently by the enemy during the whole day. The Battalion was relieved by the 15th Lancashire Fusiliers and proceeded to Billets in GERMAINE. relief complete 11.40 p.m.
			
			        CASUALTIES
			        Killed in Action
			      2nd Lieut W. Beattie
			        Wounded in Action
			      Captain A.F. Blackie	

GERMAINE	16th		In Billets GERMAINE	
GERMAINE	17th		In Billets GERMAINE Lieut R.J. Downing transferred to ENGLAND on this date.	
GERMAINE	18th		In Billets GERMAINE.	

Volume 18. page 5.

Army Form C. 2118.

WAR DIARY
or
INTELLIGENCE SUMMARY

(Erase heading not required.)

Instructions regarding War Diaries and Intelligence Summaries are contained in F. S. Regs., Part II. and the Staff Manual respectively. Title Pages will be prepared in manuscript.

Place	Date	Hour	Summary of Events and Information	Remarks and references to Appendices
GERMAINE	19th		In Billets in Divisional Reserve in GERMAINE. The Battalion was relieved by the 2/1st Bucks Regiment and proceeded to Billets in OFFOY.	
OFFOY	20th		In Billets in Corps Reserve in OFFOY.	
OFFOY	21st		In Billets in Corps Reserve in OFFOY.	
OFFOY	22nd		In Billets in Corps Reserve in OFFOY.	
OFFOY	23rd		In Billets in Corps Reserve in OFFOY.	
OFFOY	24th		In Billets in Corps Reserve in OFFOY.	
OFFOY	25th		In Billets in Corps Reserve in OFFOY.	
OFFOY	26th		In Billets in Corps Reserve in OFFOY.	
OFFOY	27th		In Billets in Corps Reserve in OFFOY.	
OFFOY	28th		In Billets in Corps Reserve in OFFOY.	
OFFOY	29th		In Billets in Corps Reserve in OFFOY.	

SECRET.   16th (Service) Battalion H.L.I.

OPERATION ORDER.

The 2nd K.O.Y.L.I. and the 16th H.L.I. will attack the town of FAYET and beyond on the night of 13/14th April, 1917.

Zero will be at 4-30 a.m.

The 2nd K.O.Y.L.I. on the left and the 16th High L.I. on the right.

The Battalion will parade on the road opposite their bivouacs ready to move off at 1-30 a.m. in the following order :
A B, C, D Companies.

They will be formed up on the position of assembly ready to attack 15 minutes before Zero.

B and A Companies will form the first two waves. B Company on the right and A Company on the left.

Each Company frontage will be 250 yards.

C and D Companies will form the second two waves., D Company on the right and C Company on the left.

The Company formation as laid down in S.S.143 2ill be adopted. The distance between the second and third waves will be 100 yards. The centre of the advance will be on a bearing of 74 degrees true.

If any dug-outs are met with these must be dealt with by men specially detailed from second waves. Should enemy Machine Guns be met with, the Lewis Guns will at once engage them. O.C. Companies will take care to ensure that clear instructions are given to this. Two snipers should be detailed to accompany each Gun. Their duty will be to counter any enemy snipers who may be trying to take off the Lewis Gunners.

As soon as the first objective has been gained it will be at once consolidated and made as strong as possible.

D and C Companies will move through the first objective as soon as the barrage lifts, and should proceed to the second objective which they will attack with the utmost vigour. When this has been captured a heavy fire from Rifles and Lewis Guns will be opened on the enemy on front, who will be retreating, and also in the direction of CEPY FARM.

When C and D Companies have gained the second objective B and A Companies will swing round and consolidate the position running from S.5.d.5.6. to S.6.a.3.3. (1/20,000) forming the defensive flank to the South East.

It is imperative that B and A Companies as soon as they have obtained the first objective will at once open fire till the succeeding waves pass through, whether they have a target or not. This will have the effect of keeping the enemy's heads down, but should an enemy Machine Gun disclose itself, not only the Lewis Guns as above ordered but all available Rifles will be concentrated on it, and knock it out. On reaching the second objective, a patrol of 20 men under an Officer will be sent out to reconnoitre to the East up to the edge of the 120 contour, and report as to whether there are any enemy trenches, and whether there is any trace of them.

Each Bombing Section will be complete with its full complement of Bombs.

50 flares will be issued per Company. These will be employed to indicate the position of the Infantry when called for by an Aeroplane.

The men will be in fighting Order, and will carry :-
Pick or Shovel.
170 rounds S.A.A., with the exception of the Bombers, Scouts, Lewis Gunners, Signallers and Messengers, who will carry 50 rounds each.
The unexpired portion of the day's rations, and Iron Rations, with Water Bottles full.
Greatcoats will be collected and put in separate bundles, marked and dumped at Battalion Headquarters in HOWLON WOOD.

road in S.4.c. or in such position on the right flank as may prove suitable, and bring fire to bear on FAYET, and the right flank of the attack., and also on the second objective of the 16th High.L.I.

One section will be held in reserve.

As soon as the second objective has been captured two sections from the Group about the road in S.4.c. will be sent forward to positions in the line captured by the 16th High.L.I.

One Section from the right Group, one Section from the left Group and one Section in reserve will be sent forward to positions in the line captured by 2nd K.O.Y.L.I.

11th Border Regiment will supply the necessary carrying parties in consultation with O.C. 97th M.G. Company.

TRENCH MORTAR BATTERY.

2 Guns will be attached to each of the assaulting Battalions and will assemble with them.

The Battery will find its own carrying parties from the remainder.

They will move behind the assaulting Companies and will come into action immediately, on their own initiative, should the attack be held up.

ARTILLERY.

The Artillery will support the attack on both objectives by placing a barrage in front of the assaulting troops as follows :-

Zero.
Infantry advances.
All Guns open a barrage which will creep at the rate of 50 yards a minute.
Plus 16 minutes.
Barrage reaches village and commences to creep at 25 yards a minute to first objective.
Plus 48 minutes.
Guns lift off first objective to line of second objective.
Plus 58 minutes.
Infantry advances to second objective.
At the same time a barrage creeping at the rate of 50 yards per minute moves in front of the two left Companies 2nd K.O.Y.L.I. to a line just short of the TWIN COPSES in M.28 and 29.
Plus 1 hour and 10 minutes.
Barrage in front of two left Companies 2nd K.O.Y.L.I. slows down and cease at plus 1 hour and 20 minutes.
Plus 1 hour 18 minutes.
Guns lift off second objective to road exits from FAYET and on to CEPY FARM, at the same time protecting the N. flank.

COMMUNICATIONS.

The Battalions will arrange to provide telephonic communication to their advanced Companies as soon as possible after Zero. Visual signalling stations will also be established and a chain of runners posted along telephone lines as arranged for in attack on SAVY.

A Contact Aeroplane will fly over the line at a time to be notified later.

Flares will be shown when called for. One flare per man will be carried by the assaulting troops.

NUMBER OF OFFICERS and SPECIALISTS to ACCOMPANY UNITS.

Not more than 20 Officers per Battalion will accompany Units in the attack.

A proportion of N.C.O's (including Company Sergeant-Majors) and specialists will be left behind.

SYNCHRONISATION of WATCHES.
Watches will be syncronised at Advanced Brigade Hq. three hours before Zero.

HEADQUARTERS.

Brigade Headquarters will be established in X.18.a. three Hours before Zero.

ADMINISTRATIVE ARRANGEMENTS.

Separate instructions will be issued as to Medical Arrangements, Stragglers Posts, and Prisoners of War.

[signature: McFarlane]
Lieut. & Adjutant,
16th (Service) Battalion H.L.I.,

11th April, 1917.

- 2 -

O.C. Companies will ensure that men are provided with a substantially hot meal at midnight.

O.C. Companies will each detail four messengers to report at head of column at 1-30 a.m.

Each O.C. Company will have one messenger from each platoon attached to his Company Headquarters.

Macfarlane
Lieut. & Adjutant,

16th (Service) Battalion H.L.I.,

13th April, 1917.

Vol 18

18.P.
8 sheets

War Diary
of the
16th Battalion Highland Light Infantry
Volume 19.
From 1st to 31st May. 1917.

Confidential

18.P.
8 sheets

Army Form C. 2118.

VOLUME 19. PAGE 1.

Instructions regarding War Diaries and Intelligence Summaries are contained in F. S. Regs., Part II. and the Staff Manual respectively. Title pages will be prepared in manuscript.

WAR DIARY
or
INTELLIGENCE SUMMARY.

(Erase heading not required.)

Place	1917 May	Hour	Summary of Events and Information	Remarks and references to Appendices
OFFOY	1st		In Billets in OFFOY. Draft of 6 Other ranks joined Battalion on this date. List of Honours and Awards granted to the Battalion are attached as Appendix 1.	
OFFOY	2nd		In Billets in OFFOY. The following Officers joined the Battalion for duty on this date :- Captain T.B. Gray from 8th H.L.I. Captain T.M. McLeod from 4th H.L.I. 2/Lieut S.M. Roberts from 4th H.L.I. 2/Lieut W.N.M. Armour from G.H.Q. Cadet School. Draft of 75 Other ranks joined Battalion for duty on this date.	
OFFOY	3rd		In Billets in OFFOY.	
OFFOY	4th		In Billets in OFFOY.	
OFFOY	5th		In Billets in OFFOY.	
OFFOY	6th		In Billets in OFFOY. Draft of 14 Other ranks joined Battalion for duty on this date.	
OFFOY	7th		In Billet in OFFOY.	
OFFOY	8th		In Billet in OFFOY.	
OFFOY	9th		In Billet in OFFOY.	
OFFOY	10th		In Billet in OFFOY. The undernoted Officer joined the Battalion for duty on this date :- Captain M.B. Fox, from 46th Infantry Brigade.	
OFFOY	11th		In Billets in OFFOY.	

Army Form C. 2118.

WAR DIARY
or
INTELLIGENCE SUMMARY.

(Erase heading not required.)

VOLUME 19. PAGE 5.

Instructions regarding War Diaries and Intelligence Summaries are contained in F. S. Regs., Part II. and the Staff Manual respectively. Title pages will be prepared in manuscript.

Place	1917. May.	Hour	Summary of Events and Information	Remarks and references to Appendices
OFFOY	12th		In Billets in OFFOY. Draft of 14 Other ranks joined Battalion for duty on the date.	
OFFOY	13th		In Billets in OFFOY.	
OFFOY	14th		In Billets in OFFOY. Casualties :- Killed (Accidentally) 1 o.r. Wounded (Accidentally) 2/Lieut P. Crichton, and 2 o.r.	
OFFOY	15th		In Billets in OFFOY. The Battalion moved from Billets in OFFOY to Billets in ETALON.	
ETALON	16th		In Billets in ETALON. The Battalion moved from Billets in ETALON to Billets in ROSIERES	
ROSIERES	17th		In Billets in ROSIERES. The Battalion moved from Billets in ROSIERES to Billets in THENNES	
THENNES	18th		In Billets in THENNES.	
THENNES	19th		In Billets in THENNES. Draft of 4 o.r. joined Battalion for duty on this date.	
THENNES	20th		In Billets in THENNES	
THENNES	21st		In Billets in THENNES	

Army Form C. 2118.

VOLUME 19. Page 3.

Instructions regarding War Diaries and Intelligence Summaries are contained in F.S. Regs., Part II. and the Staff Manual respectively. Title pages will be prepared in manuscript.

WAR DIARY
or
INTELLIGENCE SUMMARY.

(*Erase heading not required.*)

Place	Date 1917 May	Hour	Summary of Events and Information	Remarks and references to Appendices
THENNES	22nd		In Billets THENNES	any
THENNES	23rd		Letter from General Rawlinson, Commanding, IVth Army is attached as appendix 2.	any
THENNES	24th		In Billets THENNES	any
THENNES	25th		In Billets THENNES	any
THENNES	26th		In Billets THENNES	any
THENNES	27th		In Billets THENNES Draft of 3 o.r. joined Battalion on this date. The following Officers joined the Battalion on this date 2nd Lieut J. Ferris from 3rd H.L.I. 2nd Lieut W. Gray from 3rd H.L.I. 2nd Lieut D.McK. Ross from 3rd H.L.I. 2nd Lieut T.W. Hill from 3rd H.L.I.	any
THENNES	28th		In Billets THENNES.	any
THENNES	29th		In Billets THENNES.	any
THENNES	30th		In Billets THENNES.	any

Army Form C. 2118.

WAR DIARY
or
INTELLIGENCE SUMMARY.
(Erase heading not required.)

Instructions regarding War Diaries and Intelligence Summaries are contained in F. S. Regs., Part II. and the Staff Manual respectively. Title pages will be prepared in manuscript.

Place	Date 1917	Hour	Summary of Events and Information	Remarks and references to Appendices
	May.			army
	30th		At 8 a.m. the Battalion moved to billets in CACHY.	army
CACHY	31st		In billets in CACHY.	

R. Kyme, Lieut-Colonel,
Commanding 16th (Service) Battalion H.L.I.,

Appendix 11.

Fourth Army No. G.S.702.

32nd Division.

As the Division will shortly be leaving the Fourth Army I desire to express to all ranks my warm thanks for the excellent services they have performed whilst under my Command. The gallantry and dash displayed by the Division during the advance in March and April, especially in the actions resulting in the capture of SAVY, BOIS de SAVY, FRANCILLY, HOLNON, SELENCY, FAYET and CEPY FARM, reflect the highest credit on all concerned.

The skilful leadership of all ranks, coupled with the close co-operation between Artillery, Infantry and Aircraft, was a feature in these operations deserving the highest praise, and I heartily congratulate the Division on the successes they have achieved.

I much regret that the Division is now leaving the Fourth Army, but I shall hope that at some future date I may again have the good fortune to find them under my Command.

H.Q., Fourth Army,
22nd May, 1917.

H. Rawlinson
General,
Commanding Fourth Army.

Vol 19

19.P.
4 sheets

- W A R   D I A R Y -

...of the...

16th (Service) Battalion The Highland Light Infantry.

VOLUME XX.

From 1st to 30th JUNE, 1917.

Army Form C. 2118.

WAR DIARY
or
INTELLIGENCE SUMMARY.
(Erase heading not required.)

Instructions regarding War Diaries and Intelligence Summaries are contained in F. S. Regs., Part II. and the Staff Manual respectively. Title pages will be prepared in manuscript.

Place	Date 1917 June	Hour	Summary of Events and Information	Remarks and references to Appendices
CACHY	1st		In Billets, CACHY. Move from Billets in CACHY and entrain at VILLERS BRETTONEUX to Billets in the DOULIEU Area.	nil
DOULIEU	2nd		In Billets, DOULIEU Area	nil
DOULIEU	3rd		In Billets, DOULIEU Area	nil
DOULIEU	4th		In Billets, DOULIEU Area. Draft of 30 other ranks joined the Battalion for duty.	nil
DOULIEU	5th		In Billets, DOULIEU Area. Draft of 24 other ranks joined the Battalion for duty	nil
DOULIEU	6th		In Billets, DOULIEU Area	nil
DOULIEU	7th		In Billets, DOULIEU Area. The undernoted officer having been transferred to England is struck off strength from to-day's date. 2nd Lieut. W.N. ARMOUR.	nil
DOULIEU	8th		In Billets, DOULIEU Area.	nil
DOULIEU	9th		In Billets, DOULIEU Area	nil
DOULIEU	10th		In Billets, DOULIEU Area	nil
DOULIEU	11th		In Billets DOULIEU Area. The undernoted officer having been transferred to 2/7th Duke of Wellington's Regt is struck off strength from to-day's date. 2nd Lieut. C.G. STOTT	nil
DOULIEU	12th		In Billets, DOULIEU Area. 1 other ranks joined the Battalion for duty	nil

2353 Wt.W2541/1454 700,000 5/15 D. D. & L. A.D.S.S./Forms/C. 2118.

WAR DIARY
or
INTELLIGENCE SUMMARY.
(Erase heading not required.)

Army Form C. 2118.

Instructions regarding War Diaries and Intelligence Summaries are contained in F. S. Regs., Part II. and the Staff Manual respectively. Title pages will be prepared in manuscript.

Place	1917 June Date	Hour	Summary of Events and Information	Remarks and references to Appendices
DOULIEU	13th		In Billets, DOULIEU Area	nil
DOULIEU	14th		In Billets, DOULIEU Area. March to Billets in the EECKE Area	nil
EECKE	15th		In Billets, EECKE Area	nil
EECKE	16th		In Billets, EECKE Area. Move from Billets in EECKE Area by bus to Billets in PETIT SYNTHE	nil
PETIT SYNTHE	17th		In Billets, PETIT SYNTHE	nil
PETIT SYNTHE	18th		In Billets PETIT SYNTHE March to DUNKERQUE, and move by train to Hutments in Camp JUNIAC.	nil
Camp JUNIAC	19th		In Hutments CAMP JUNIAC. Relieve the French in the Coast Line Defences, Route EOLIENNE (exclusive) to LA PANNE BAINS (exclusive). Relief complete - 9.30 p.m.	nil
Camp JUNIAC	20th		In Hutments, Camp JUNIAC	nil
Camp JUNIAC	21st		In Hutments, CAMP JUNIAC. Draft of 7 other ranks joined the Battalion for duty	nil
Camp JUNIAC	22nd		In hutments, Camp JUNIAC.	nil

VOLUME. 20. Page. 3.

WAR DIARY
or
INTELLIGENCE SUMMARY.
(Erase heading not required.)

Army Form C. 2118.

16 HLI
9/61

Place	1917. June.	Hour	Summary of Events and Information	Remarks and references to Appendices
Camp JUNIAC.	23rd.		In Hutments, Camp JUNIAC. The King's Royal Rifles take over the Coast Line Defences. Relief complete - 9.30 p.m.	
Camp JUNIAC.	24th		In Hutments Camp JUNIAC. The undernoted Officers joined the Battalion from the 3rd H.L.I. 2nd Lieut. W. FINGLAND. 2nd Lieut. D. M. ROBERTSON.	
Camp JUNIAC.	25th		In Hutments, Camp JUNIAC. Move from Camp JUNIAC to Brigade Support in NIEUPORT.	
NIEUPORT.	26th		In Billets, NIEUPORT. 1 other ranks killed.	
NIEUPORT.	27th		In Billets, NIEUPORT. 1 other ranks wounded.	
NIEUPORT.	28th		In Billets, NIEUPORT. 6 other ranks wounded. 1 other ranks killed.	
NIEUPORT.	29th		In Billets, NIEUPORT. 2 other ranks wounded. Relieve the 2nd K.O.Y.L.I. in the Right Sub-sector (LOMBARTZYDE Sector) Relief complete. - 12.40 a.m. 30th June, 1917.	
Right Sub-Sector.	30th		In occupation of Right Sub-sector. LOMBARTZYDE Sector.	

Lieut-Colonel,
Commanding

Nov 20
91/32

20.P.
15 sheets

War Diary

of the

16th (Service) Bn Highland Light Infantry

Volume 21

1st to 31st July, 1917.

Army Form C. 2118.

WAR DIARY
or
INTELLIGENCE SUMMARY.
(Erase heading not required.)

Volume 21 page 1.

Instructions regarding War Diaries and Intelligence Summaries are contained in F. S. Regs., Part II. and the Staff Manual respectively. Title pages will be prepared in manuscript.

Place	1917. July	Hour	Summary of Events and Information	Remarks and references to Appendices
LOMBARD-ZYDE	1st		In occupation of LOMBARDZYDE Sector, Right Subsector.	—
	2nd		In occupation of LOMBARDZYDE Sector, Right Subsector. Casualties :- Killed 5 o.r. Wounded 14 o.r.	—
	3rd		In occupation of LOMBARDZYDE Sector Right Subsector.	—
	4th		In occupation of LOMBARDZYDE Sector, Right Subsector. Wounded T.B. Gray 13 o.r. The Battalion was relieved by 2nd K.O.Y.L.I. relief complete 11 p.m. On completion of relief the Battalion withdrew to Brigade Support in NIEUPORT.	—
NIEUPORT	5th		In Brigade Support NIEUPORT. Casualties Killed 2 o.r. Wounded 10 o.r. Wounded and Missing 1 o.r. "A" Company carried out a successful raid on enemy trenches at point M.23.a.3.4. Operation Orders and report are attached as appendices 1 and 2.	—
	6th		In Brigade Support NIEUPORT Casualties Wounded 1 o.r.	—
	7th		In Brigade Support NIEUPORT The following reinforcements joined the Battalion on this date :- 2/Lieut C.N. RUTHERFURD ⎫ From 5th H.L.I. 2/Lieut M.M. WOTHERSPOON ⎭ 33 Other ranks.	—
	8th		The Battalion relieved the 2nd Bn K.O.Y.L.I. in LOMBARDZYDE Sector, Right Subsector Relief complete 11.30 p.m. Casualties :- Killed 1 o.r. Wounded 5 o.r.	—
LOMBARD-ZYDE	9th		In occupation of LOMBARDZYDE Sector, Right Subsector. Casualties Killed 2 o.r. Wounded 5 o.r.	—
	10th		In occupation of LOMBARDZYDE Sector. Right Subsector. Our Sector was subjected to a violent bombardment lasting 15 hours, a special report is attached as appendix III Casualties :- Killed W. Hill, Lieut W. Greig, C.N Rutherfurd 49 o.r. 2/Lieut J.D. ROSS & J. Halliday J.W. Greig, C.N Rutherfurd 49 o.r.	—

Army Form C. 2118.

WAR DIARY
or
INTELLIGENCE SUMMARY.
(Erase heading not required.)

page 2.

Place	1917. July	Hour	Summary of Events and Information	Remarks and references to Appendices
LOMBARD-ZYDE	11th		In occupation of LOMBARDZYDE Sector Right SubSector. Casualties Killed 11 o.r. Wounded 56 o.r. Missing 9 o.r.	any
	12th		The Battalion was relieved by the 2nd Manchesters and moved to Hutments in JEAN BART Camp, COXYDE. Relief complete 3.30 a.m. Draft of 56 o.r. joined Battalion this date.	any
JEAN BART CAMP.	13th		In Hutments JEAN BART Camp. Casualties Wounded 2 o.r.	any
	14th		In Hutments JEAN BART CAMP	any
	15th		In Hutments JEAN BART CAMP	any
	16th		In HUTMENTS JEAN BART CAMP. The Battalion moved from Hutments in JEAN BART Camp to Hutments in GHYVELDE	any
GHYVELDE	17th		In Hutments in GHYVELDE	any
	18th		In Hutments GHYVELDE. Draft of 21 or joined Battalion this date	any
	19th		In Hutments GHYVELDE	any
	20th		In Hutments GHYVELDE. The Battalion moved from GHYVELDE to Camp in D.8.a. BRAY DUNES Area	any
	21st		Under Canvas in Camp D.8.a. BRAY DUNES Area.	any
	22nd		Under Canvas in Camp D.8.a. Bray Dunes Area. Draft of 102 o.r. joined Battalion this date.	any
	23rd		Under Canvas in Camp D.8.a. Bray Dunes Area. List of Honours and awards granted during this month is attached as appendix 4.	any
	24th		Under Canvas in Camp D.8.a. BRAY DUNES Area	any
	25th		Under Canvas in Camp D.8.a. BRAY DUNES Area. Draft of 8 o.r. Joined Battalion this date.	any

Page 3.

Army Form C. 2118.

WAR DIARY
or
INTELLIGENCE SUMMARY.
(Erase heading not required.)

Instructions regarding War Diaries and Intelligence Summaries are contained in F. S. Regs., Part II. and the Staff Manual respectively. Title pages will be prepared in manuscript.

Place	Date 1917 July	Hour	Summary of Events and Information	Remarks and references to Appendices
Camp D.8.a.	26th		Under canvas in Camp D.8.a. BRAY DUNES Area.	nil.
	27th		Under canvas in Camp D.8.a. BRAY DUNES Area The Battalion moved from Camp D.8.a. to KUHN Camp, Coxyde.	nil.
KUHN Camp	28th		In Hutments 2 o.r. Wounded KUHN Camp	nil.
	29th		In Hutments KUHN Camp Casualties Wounded 2 o.r.	nil.
	30th		In Hutments KUHN Camp	nil.
	31st		In Hutments KUHN Camp Casualties Wounded 1 o.r.	nil.
			Congratulatory messages are attached as appendices 5 and 6.	

Lieut Colonel,
Commanding, 16th Highland Light Infantry

Appendix 3

Report on the Operations of 16th Battalion
The Highland Light Infantry in the NIEUPORT Area,
"C" Sector, Right Sub-sector, 8/11th July, 1917.

----

1. The 16th Battalion The Highland Light Infantry relieved 2nd Battalion K.O.Y.L.I., in "C" Sector, RIGHT Sub-sector, on the night of 8/9th July, 1917.

9/7/17.
2. Artillery activity on both sides was normal on 9th July till 6.30 p.m. when our Guns fired Scheme X. lasting till 7.20 p.m.

3. At 11.45 p.m. 9/7/17, the enemy opened barrage fire on the left- sub-sector, thence spreading to first three lines of Right Sub-sector, ending at 12.45 a.m. 10/7/17. There were about 400 men working in our First Line, with cover for less than 100, and numerous casualties were taken.

10/7/17.

4. A Strafing Patrol (1 N.C.O. and 8 men with Lewis Gun) went out from M.23.a.2.2. at 1.15 a.m., returning at 2 a.m. Listening Posts were also out from dusk to dawn. No enemy was seen in "No man's Land", but the enemy could be heard very busy in his front line.

5. At 6.45 a.m. the enemy opened on our front First, Second, and Third Lines with T.M's. This fire gradually increased in intensity, until it developed into a violent bombardment of all our lines from Guns and Howitzers of all calibres, which lasted until 9.30 p.m. There were observational intervals at 12.45 p.m., 3.25 p.m., 6 p.m., and 7.40 p.m., during which enemy Aeroplanes flew at a low altitude up and down our lines, without interference. except from L.G. and Rifle Fire.

6. By 10 a.m. all wires were cut and communication thereafter was only by runners. The communication trenches between first and third lines were impassable, and access to the front line was only possible over the open. The 2" T.M. Battery in our Second Line was out of action, all guns and ammunition being buried. Our First Line was considerably damaged, but still tenable. Two strong points, one in centre, and one on left flank at junction with NOSE AVENUE, were held continuously, and the other posts were constantly re-organised, as the enemy's fire made necessary. During the whole time our men preserved vigilance.

7. Throughout this day there was no communication with the Battalion on the left, and it was only at 10 p.m. that word was received that an enemy patrol had entered their front line.

2.

8. At 1.25 p.m. "B" Company of the 2nd K.O.Y.L.I. reported and was sent to reinforce garrison of third line (NASAL TRENCH). At 2.25 p.m. "A" Company, 2nd K.O.Y.L.I. reported. Two platoons were sent to NASAL SUPPORT and two to NASAL LANE.

9. When the bombardment ceased at 9.30 p.m. NOSE TRENCH, NOSE SUPPORT, NASAL WALK, and communication trenches were practically levelled. Casualties were roughly estimated up to this time at 150.

10. The disposition at 9.30 p.m. was -
    1st Line : 2 Platoons, 16th High.L.I.
    2nd Line : 4 Platoons, 16th High.L.I.

    3rd Line : 2 Platoons, 16th High.L.I.
               2 Companies, 2nd K.O.Y.L.I.

    4th Line : 2 Companies, 16th High.L.I.
               1 Company, 2nd K.O.Y.L.I.

11. At 10 p.m. the first line was reinforced from the second. A Battle Patrol and two Listening Posts were pushed out into "No Man's Land" and remained there till dawn.

12. At 10.30 p.m. many gas shells (Lethal) fell on our fourth line, and round Battalion Headquarters.

11/7/17.   13. At 5 a.m. (11/7/17). touch was secured with 16th North'd Fusrs. in Fourth Line of Left Sub-sector.

14. The disposition at 7 a.m. (11/7/17). was :-

    1st Line : 9 Posts, 2 Platoons, 16th H.L.I.
    2nd Line : 7 Posts, 4 platoons, 16th H.L.I.
              2 Vickers Guns, 2 Stokes Guns.

    3rd Line : 2 Platoons, 16th High.L.I.
               2 Companies, 2nd K.O.Y.L.I.
    of which two Platoons were extended into left sub-sector.

    4th Line : 2 Companies, 16th High.L.I.
               1 Company, 2nd K.O.Y.L.I.

15. At 8a.m. enemy T.M's opened on our first and second lines. From 8 to 9 a.m. enemy Aeroplanes were active over all our lines. At 9.35 a.m. enemy guns opened on our front line and were active all day, though the fire was not so intense as on the previous day.

16. At 10 a.m. two platoons, 2nd K.O.Y.L.I. were sent up to reinforce garrison of second Line. One platoon, 2nd K.O.Y.L.I. was ordered to reinforce garrison of left sub-sector. Heavy shelling with aerial observation prevented these movements being executed.

3.

17. At 8.30 p.m. a patrol was sent into Left Sub-sector, and got touch with 16th North'd Fusrs. who were then holding the second line.

Another patrol proceeded along First Line of Left Sub-sector as far as the Right Post, which was then unoccupied, and could find no trace of the enemy. It was impossible to go further, the whole breastwork being levelled.

18. The 16th H.L.I. were relieved by the 2nd Manchester Regiment on night of 11/12th July, 1917. Whilst relief was in progress the enemy opened a violent barrage fire at 10.30 p.m. on our Third Line, spreading to all other lines. The S.O.S. was sent up, but not repeated, as quiet was restored in ten minutes, and no infantry attack was reported. From midnight 11/12th July to 5 a.m. 12/7/17 many Gas Shells, (Lethal) fell in vicinity of Battalion Headquarters.

19. Casualties of 16th High.L.I. during tour of duty 8/11th July, 1917, were :

    <u>Killed</u> : Officer, 1 ; o.r. 22.

    <u>Wounded</u> : Officers 4 ; o.r. 112.

  <u>Wounded and Missing</u> (Believed Killed), o.r. 5

    <u>Total</u> : Officers, 5 o.r. 140.

20. The feature of the operations most worrying to the garrison was the constant observation by enemy Aeroplanes, who noted every move in our dispositions.

21. The 3 Companies ("A" "B" and "D") of the 2nd K.O.Y.L.I. which reinforced the 16th High.L.I. carried out the duties assigned to them with commendable efficiency. The 97th Trench Mortar Battery gave valuable assistance in the defence of the sub-sector, until their guns were completely buried by hostile shell fire.

22. Our Lewis Guns were active throughout. At one time three out of the four Lewis Guns in the first line were out of action, owing to shell fire, but these were promptly replaced.

23. The garrison were fortunate in having sand-bags as revetments, as after each bombardment they were able quickly to build up fresh cover.

24. During the whole of the operations the strictest discipline was maintained. The officers, N.C.O's and men of the 16th High.L.I. preserved unceasing vigilance under exceedingly trying conditions. The Posts in the first line were relieved three times during the tour of duty.

W E Gamss Fisher
Captain.
Intelligence Officer,
16th High.L.I.

14th July, 1917.

ix. 4

The Field Marshal Commander-in-Chief, under
...rity granted by His Majesty the King, has awarded the
...ing decorations :-

The Military Cross.
2nd Lieut. D. F. Brodie.

The Distinguished Conduct Medal.
No. 14173 Sergt. J. Girdwood.

The Military Medal.
No. 8752 Pte. J. Keenan.
No. 3393 Pte. D. McKay.
No. 17656 L/Cpl. H. Harrison.
No. 3627 Pte. W. Copeland.
No. 3532 Pte. A. Walker.
No. 1390 L/Cpl. J. Forbes.
No. 14120 Cpl. G. Berry.
No. 1481 Pte. J. Hogg.
No. 43034 Cpl. W. Imrie
No. 14140 Sgt. H. J. Cross.
No. 34093 Pte. T. Simpson.
No. 14306 Pte. D. Wilkie.
No. 1371 Pte. T. Swan.

Appendix. 5.

The Field Marshal, Commanding in Chief, visited the Divisional Commander yesterday and expressed his appreciation of the fine fighting of the 32nd Division during the recent operations in the LOMBARTZYDE and ST. GEORGE'S Sectors.

The Divisional Commander has great pleasure in conveying to all ranks the congratulations of the Commander in Cheif, and is confident that the Division will continue to maintain the high reputation it has earned for itself.

                    (Signed) A E. MACNAMARA,
                          Lieut-Colonel,
                          General Staff, 32nd Division.

27th July, 1917.

Appendix. 6.

      The Corps Commander directs me to convey to you his appreciation of the gallantry and devotion to duty displayed by all ranks under the most difficult conditions in the defence of the YSER Bridge Head.

      The Royal Flying Corps and Royal Artillery by their efforts have ably supported the Infantry of the 1st and 32nd Divisions, whose action during the battle of July, 10th. was in accordance with the highest traditions of the British Infantry. The Royal Engineers have distinguished themselves by their unceasing work in maintaining the bridges over the Yser, while the work of Medical Units is dserving of the highest praise.

      The Corps Commander wishes his appreciation conveyed to all ranks under your Command.

      (Signed) H. KNOX,
          Brigadier-General.
          General Staff,
          15th Corps.

15th July, 1917.

Ref. 16/97.

...TION ORDER :

... at approximately M.23.a.3.4., will
... the night of 4/5th July, 1917.

:-

...troy by demolition M.G. emplacements
... has any gas installed in his front
...rs to establish identification.
...ints at (Y) with high explosive.
...over of a three minute burst of
...me table :-

... be for ed up N. of ditch running in
...pens on front line
...ry ceases and raiding party advances.
...rage commences.
...ge ceases, and guns on front line
... ceases fire.

...out by "A" Company who will detail

...mmand.
...O.C. Raiding Party.

...ed as follows :-

...other ranks.
...nt "B" 1 N.C.O. and 6 men.)
...nt "C" 1 N.C.O. and 6 men.)
...ieut. Brodie and 12 other ranks.
...ther ranks.
... be on duty in the Sector, and will

...n.
...ners.
...ed.

...ain McLeod of the position he will occup...
... stand by ready to assist the raiding
...idson will order these to fire

..."No Man's Land" in front of our
..." half an hour before zero.
...ve point one hour before zero.
...ther the wire is sufficinetly cut
...g through, and will have the party
...awal can be effected should the wire
... will carry two duckw lks, which will
... cross any uncut knife rests.
...he party will enter the trench at
... A block will be formed about 20 yards

... entered a party will proceed to

... deal with the dug-outs marked "X"
...Gun emplacement in "Y"

2.

(iv) DRESS

Rifle and Bayonet with rounds in magazine, and two clips in left pocket. Two bombs will be taken in the right pocket, and the N.C.O. and 6 men who are to form block "B" will each carry 6 bombs in sandbags as a reserve. Two of this party will cut wire and widen the gate if necessary. Steel helmets will be worn, and faces will be darkened. All identification marks will be removed, and no papers or maps will be carried by any of the party.

(v) DEMOLITION.

A party of 2 other ranks will carry high explosive charge for the purpose of wrecking the concrete work marked "Y" on plan. Orders for setting off this charge will be given by 2nd Lieut. BRODIE when he has ascertained that all the parties have withdrawn.

(vi) WITHDRAWAL.

The parties will withdraw immediate,y their tasks are completed, or, if not completed, whenever the bugle sounds. Two buglers will be with Captain McLeod who will give orders for the sounding of the bugle. Men will be detailed to carry back any wounded.

When the withdrawal is taking place, if the enemy shelling is active on our front, the party will take cover on the bank of the stream running in front of our line.

(vii) PRISONERS.

No more than 4 prisoners should be taken, and these will be brought back to Battalion Headquarters, the escort taking care that they do not destroy any papers. Prisoners will then be immediately sent on to Brigade Headquarters.

5. Sketch Map has already been issued to O.C. Raiding Party.

6. Watches will be synchronised at Battalion Headquarters at 6 p.m. and 10 p.m. on 4th inst.

7. The Commanding Officer will be present at Battalion Headquarters from 1.30 a.m. on 5th until the Raiding Party returns.

8. Captain McLeod will render a report on the operation to reach Battalion Headquarters as soon as possible after his party returns.

9. A C K N O W L E D G E.

Macfarlane
Lieut. & Adjutant,

16th (Service) Battalion High.L.I.,

3rd July, 1917.
Issued at 12 midnight.

Copies to -
1. Captain. McLeod.
2. 2nd Lieut. Brodie.
3. Captain Davidson.
4. 97th Infantry Brigade.
5. 2d K.O.Y.L.I.
6. Commanding Officer.
7. File.

Appendix 2

Ref. 16/130.

To : Headquarters,
       97th Infantry Brigade.

Report on "B" Raid on point M.23.a.1.3. by 16th Battalion The Highland Light Infantry, on night of 4/5th July, 1917.

Ref. annexed sketch Map, 1/333.

1. This raid was carried out by a special party consisting of Captain T.M. McLeod, 2nd Lieut. D. F. Brodie, and 34 other ranks. from "A" Company, 16th High.L.I.

2. Dress : Rifle and Bayonet with 10 rounds in magazine, and two clips in left pocket. 2 Mill No. 5 Grenades in right pocket. One N.C.O. and 6 men to form blocking party carried 6 Mill's No. 5 Grenades per man in bucket as reserve. Steel Helmets will be worn, and faces blackened. All identification marks were removed. No papers or maps were carried.

3. Captain T.M. McLeod in Command of the raid with 4 other ranks took position in NOSE TRENCH at point M.23.a.1.1.

4. 2nd Lieut. D.F. Brodie with 28 other ranks took up position in front of BOTERBEEK Brook, running parallel to our front at a distance of 20 yards, at 1.15 a.m.

5. "No Man's Land" at this point is about 80 yards wide, in good condition but for shell holes. covered with long grass.

6. ZERO time was 1.45 a.m. at which hour the Artillery bombardment opened on German front line. At 1.48 a.m. the bombardment ceased, and the raiding party advanced in single file to the gap in enemy wire already reconnoitered at point "A" This gap was about 3 yards wide. As the party entered it a shell burst close by, causing casualties 1 killed and 1 seriously wounded. This caused a temporary delay while the gap was cleared.

7. At 1.49 a.m. the box barrage commenced. 2nd Lieut. Brodie with his party advanced up the gentle slope leading to top of parapet. He there saw a German sentry in the trench midway between "A" and "B" and shot him with his revolver. Seeing no other enemy in the trenches he then ran across the parapet to dug-out "X" and hearing voices from it ordered it to be bombed. 8 Mill's No. 5 Grenades were thrown in screams rapidly dying away were heard, and no survivors were seen on inspection. Probably 9 or 10 men had taken shelter from our bombardment in this dug-out, which was about 10 feet long and 8 feet wide.

2.

8. 2nd Lieut. Brodie and No. 17650 L/Cpl. Harrison meanwhile jumped across the trench to roof of dug-out "Y" they saw a German at point "D" aiming a rifle, and L/Cpl. Harrison shot him. 2 Mill's No. 5 Grenades were thrown into dug-out "Y" inside which 6 or 7 Germans were seen. This appears from statement of prisoner to have been the German Platoon Commander's Dug-out, inside which he seems to have taken shelter whith his HTQs. and some other ranks. There were no survivors.

9. It had been intended to blow up this dug-out with gun-cotton. The man with the fuze, however, had become a casualty, and the demolition was abandoned. The dug-out was merely an ordinary shelter. and M.G. or emplacement of any kind could be seen.

10. The party then proceeded along the trench towards point "C" a blocking party having been left as arranged at point "B" Several of the enemy were met in this trench. Three were made prisoners and the rest were bayoneted.

11. A considerable number of the enemy appeared to be forming up in trench "C" from which they were throwing bombs in large numbers, causing several casualties. Time being now up, 2nd Lieut. Brodie withdrew his party.

12. A German was seen in trench at point "E" Being summoned to surrender, he advanced with hands up. and was escorted back to our lines. The other three prisoners attempted to escape were killed. A Greatcoat and set of equipment were brought back.

13. The raiding party returned to our trenches at point M.23.a.1.1. at 2.6 a.m.

14. Our casualties : 2 Killed 10 wounded, 1 wounded and Missing. The missing man is known to have been brought back to ur lines, but has not yet reported. The inference is that he must have been blown to pieces or buried during the heavy bombardment of our lines which followed immediately on return of Raiding party, and lasted until 4 a.m.

15. Estimated enemy casualties : Killed 1 Officer and 17 other ranks. Wounded 6 other ranks, Prisoners 1 other rank. Total 1 Officer and 24 other ranks.

16. Enemy Dug-outs. Dug-out "X" is about 10 feet long by 8 feet wide, and 7 feet high (same height as parapet from ground level). Revetted outside with timber same as trenches. Entrance 4 feet high 3 feet wide.
   Dug-out "Y" is about 12 feet long by 8 feet wide, built of bricks strengthened with concrete, on site of ruined house, and lined with smooth cement. Roof slightly arched of Ferro-concrete. No emplacements or loopholes. This is a strong shelter calculated to resist anything less than a 6 inch shell. No damage had been done to either dug-out by our fire.

17. Enemy trenches: A gentle slope leads up to top of parapet. Trenches are about 9 feet deep inside and 3 feet wide. Parados is a breastwork about 7 feet above ground level. to North of trench. Revetted with continuous timbering strengthened with square posts about three feet apart. Duckboarded and in good condition

3.

-----

18. <u>Enemy gas installation.</u>   Nil.
19. <u>Enemy M.G.'s or emplacements.</u>   <u>Nil.</u>

(Signed) W.E. GARRETT-FISHER,
Captain, for
Lieut-Colonel, Commanding 16th High.L.I.

6th July, 1917.
12 noon.

Vol 21

H.P.
9 sheets

- W A R D I A R Y -

... of the ...

16th Battalion The Highland Light Infantry.

VOLUME XXI.

From 1st to 31st AUGUST, 1917.

Army Form C. 2118.

Volume 22, Page 1.

WAR DIARY
or
INTELLIGENCE SUMMARY.

(Erase heading not required.)

Instructions regarding War Diaries and Intelligence Summaries are contained in F.S. Regs., Part II. and the Staff Manual respectively. Title pages will be prepared in manuscript.

Place	Date	Hour	Summary of Events and Information	Remarks and references to Appendices
	August, 1917			
KHUN CAMP	1st.		In Billets, KHUN CAMP. Divisional Reserve. 1 other ranks wounded.	any
do.	2nd.		In Hutments, KHUN CAMP. Divisional Reserve.	any
do.	3rd.		In Hutments, KHUN CAMP. Divisional Reserve.	any
do.	4th		In Hutments, KHUN CAMP. Divisional Reserve.	any
do.	5th		In Hutments, KHUN CAMP. Divisional Reserve. 8 other ranks joined the Battalion from 21st I.B.D.	any
do.	6th		In Hutments, KHUN CAMP. Divisional Reserve.	any
do.	7th		In Hutments, KHUN CAMP. Divisional Reserve.	any
do.	8th		In Hutments, KHUN CAMP. Divisional Reserve.	any
do.	9th		In Hutments, KHUN CAMP. Divisional Reserve.	any
do	10th		In Hutments, KHUN CAMP. Divisional Reserve. Relieved by 17th H...I., and march to Hutments, in JEANNIOT CAMP.	any
JEANNIOT CAMP	11th		In Hutments, JEANNIOT CAMP. Capt..in J. Alexander reported for duty with the Battalion. Lieut. C. V. Durrard, Highland Cyclist Battalion, reported for duty with the Battalion.	any
do.	12th		In Hutments, JEANNIOT CAMP.	any
do.	13th		In Hutments, JEANNIOT CAMP. 2nd Lieut. I.H. Smith, 3rd H.L. Il reported for duty with the Battalion.	any
do.	14th		In Hutments, JEANNIOT CAMP.	any

Army Form C. 2118.

WAR DIARY
or
INTELLIGENCE SUMMARY.
(Erase heading not required.)

Volume 22 Page. 2.
Instructions regarding War Diaries and Intelligence Summaries are contained in F. S. Regs., Part II. and the Staff Manual respectively. Title pages will be prepared in manuscript.

Place	Date	Hour	Summary of Events and Information	Remarks and references to Appendices
	August, 1917.			
JEANNIOT CAMP.	15th		In Hutments, JEANNIOT CAMP. Relieved by the 5th Scottish Rifles, and march to Billets in BRAY DUNES.	any
BRAY DUNES.	16th		In Billets, BRAY DUNES. Draft of 9 other ranks joined the Battalion from the 21st I.B.D. 2 other ranks wounded.	any
BRAY DUNES.	17th		In Billets, BRAY DUNES.	any
BRAY DUNES.	18th		In Billets, BRAY DUNES. Relieve 2nd Worcesters in Camp "C" GHYVELDE.	any
GHYVELDE	20th		In Hutments, GHYVELDE. Draft of 4 other ranks joined the Battalion from the 21st I.B.D.	any
GHYVELDE	21st.		In Hutments, GHYVELDE.	any
GHYVELDE	22nd.		In Hutments, GHYVELDE.	any
GHYVELDE	23rd.		In Hutments, GHYVELD.	any
GHYVELDE	24th		In Hutments, GHYVELDE. Draft of 26 other ranks joined the Battalion from the 21st I.B.D.	any
GHYVELDE	25th		In Hutments, GHYVELDE. Captain A. E. McLellan, 3rd H.L.I. reported for duty with the Battalion. Captain H.F. Martin, 3rd H.L.I. reported for duty with the Battalion.	any
GHYVELDE.	26th		In Hutments, GHYVELDE.	any

Volume 22 Page 3.

Army Form C. 2118.

WAR DIARY
or
INTELLIGENCE SUMMARY.

(Erase heading not required.)

Place	Date	Hour	Summary of Events and Information	Remarks and references to Appendices
	August, 1917.			
GHYVELDE.	27th		In Hutments, GHYVELDE. March to Billets in JEANNIOT CAMP. The undernoted officers reported for duty with the Battalion :- 2nd Lieut. H. V. Jowett, Fife and Forfar Yeomanry. 2nd Lieut. D. V. Charlton, - do - 2nd Lieut. H. N Eadie, - do - 2nd Lieut. A. Elder. - do - 2nd Lieut J. W. Linn, 1st Highland Cyclist Battalion.	
JEANNIOT CAMP.	28th		In Hutments, JEANNIOT CAMP. March to Hutments in HKUN CAMP.	
HKUN CAMP.	29th		In Divisional Reserve in HKUN CAMP.	
KHUN CAMP.	30th		In Divisional Reserve in KHUN CAMP. Draft of 7 other ranks reported for duty with the Battalion from 31st I.B.D.	
KHUN CAMP.	31st		In Divisional Reserve, KHUN CAMP.	

Lieut-Colonel,
Commanding 16th Battalion High.L.I.

CONFIDENTIAL

Vol 22

21.P.(a)

War Diary.

of the

16th Battalion Highland Light Infantry

Volume XXIII

from 16th to 30th September, 1917

Army Form C. 2118.

WAR DIARY
or
INTELLIGENCE SUMMARY.
(Erase heading not required.)

Page 1.

Instructions regarding War Diaries and Intelligence Summaries are contained in F. S. Regs., Part II. and the Staff Manual respectively. Title pages will be prepared in manuscript.

Place	Date 1917 September	Hour	Summary of Events and Information	Remarks and references to Appendices
Khun Camp	1st		In Brigade Reserve, in Hutments, KHUN CAMP. 1 o.r. Killed.	—
do.	2nd		In Brigade Reserve, in Hutments, KHUN CAMP.	—
do	3rd		In Brigade Reserve, in Hutments. KHUN CAMP. The Battalion relieved the 2nd K.O.Y.L.I. in the Right Subsector ST. GEORGE'S SECTOR, with "A" Company on right and "B" Company on left, "C" Company in support and "D" Company in reserve at GROOTE LABOUR FARM. Relief complete 11.45 pm	—
ST. GEORGE'S SECTOR	4th		In occupation of Right Sub-sector, ST. GEORGE'S Sector	—
do.	5th		In occupation of Right Sub-sector, ST. GEORGE'S Sector	—
do.	6th		In occupation of Right Sub-Sector ST. GEORGE'S Sector The undermoted Officer having joined the Battalion for duty is taken on strength, and posted to "D" Company, from this date 2nd Lieut. J. THOMPSON, 5th High. L. I.	—
do	7th		In occupation of Right Subsector ST. GEORGE'S Sector 1 o.r. Killed. 1 o.r. Wounded	—
do.	8th		In occupation of Right Subsector ST. GEORGE'S Sector	—

Page 2

WAR DIARY
or
INTELLIGENCE SUMMARY.

Army Form C. 2118.

Place	Date 1917 September	Hour	Summary of Events and Information	Remarks and references to Appendices
ST GEORGE'S SECTOR	9th		In occupation of Right Sub sector, St Georges Sector 1 o.r. Wounded. The Battalion was relieved by the 17th Highr. L.I. and moved to Brigade Reserve in OOST DUNKERKE "A" "B" "C" Companies and Headquarters in OOST DUNKERKE and "D" Company in Hutments in WELLINGTON CAMP. Relief complete 12.45am 10th September	nil
OOST DUNKERKE	10th		In Brigade Reserve in OOST DUNKERKE	nil
do	11th		In Brigade Reserve in OOST DUNKERKE. The undermentioned Officer joined the Battalion on this date 2nd Lieut R.G.A. Temple	nil
do	12th		In Brigade Reserve OOST DUNKERKE 1. o.r. Wounded.	nil
do	13th		In Billets in Brigade Reserve OOST DUNKERKE	nil
do	14th		In Billets in Brigade Reserve OOST DUNKERKE	nil
do	15th		In Billets in Brigade Reserve OOST DUNKERKE 7. o.r. killed 6. o.r. wounded. Wellington Camp ("D" Company) relieved the 2nd R.O.L.I. in the left Sub-sector St GEORGE'S Sector The Battalion on the right "D" Company on the left, "B" Company in Support with "C" Company in reserve. Relief complete 7.45am.	nil

Army Form C. 2118.

Page 3

WAR DIARY
or
INTELLIGENCE SUMMARY.

(Erase heading not required.)

Instructions regarding War Diaries and Intelligence Summaries are contained in F.S. Regs., Part II. and the Staff Manual respectively. Title pages will be prepared in manuscript.

Place	Date 1917 September	Hour	Summary of Events and Information	Remarks and references to Appendices
St Georges Sector	16th		In occupation of Left Subsector St George's Sector	
Do	17th		In occupation of Left Subsector St George's Sector. 2 o.r. Killed. 5 o.r. Wounded	
Do	18th		In occupation of Left Subsector St George's Sector. Officers attached on Strength of Battalion on this date:— The undermentioned 2nd Lieut A.D. GOWANS 2nd Lieut J. WHITFIELD 2nd Lieut R. KAY.	
Do	19th		In occupation of Left Sub sector St Georges Sector	
Do	20th		In occupation of Left Sub sector St George's Sector The undermentioned Officer having been posted to R.F.C. is struck off strength Lieut M.H. McNEIL M.G. The Battalion was relieved by the 2nd Manchester Regiment, and moved to Hutments in Khun Camp. Relief complete 3.15am.	
KHUN CAMP	21/01		In Hutments in KHUN CAMP. The Battalion marched to Billets in LA PANNE	
LA PANNE	22nd		In Billets LA PANNE. The Battalion marched to FORT DE DUNES and relieved the 5th Yorks and Lancs in Coast Defence there Relief complete 10.45am The undermentioned Officers joined the Battalion on this date:— 2nd Lieuts E.J. HILLIER W. COMRIE J.P. MITCHELL	

Page 4.

Army Form C. 2118.

WAR DIARY
or
INTELLIGENCE SUMMARY.
(Erase heading not required.)

Instructions regarding War Diaries and Intelligence Summaries are contained in F. S. Regs., Part II. and the Staff Manual respectively. Title pages will be prepared in manuscript.

Place	Date 1917 September	Hour	Summary of Events and Information	Remarks and references to Appendices
FORT DE DUNES	23rd		In occupation of Coast Defences FORT DE DUNES.	—
Do	24th		The Battalion was relieved by the 3/5th Lancashire Fusiliers and moved to Billets in LA PANNE. Relief complete 1.15 pm. The following Officer joined Battalion on this date :— Lieutenant R. B. STEWART. Draft of 6 O.R.	—
LA PANNE	25th		In Billets in LA PANNE Divisional Reserve. The following Officer joined the Battalion on this date :— Captain F. W. Kidd	—
Do	26th		In Billets LA PANNE Divisional Reserve.	—
Do	27th		In Billets LA PANNE Divisional Reserve.	—
Do	28th		In Billets LA PANNE Divisional Reserve. The Battalion relieved the 18th Northumberland Fusiliers in NIEUPORT (NEW PARADE) Relief complete 11.30 pm.	—
NIEUPORT	29th		In Brigade Reserve NEW PORADE, NIEUPORT	—
Do	30th		In Brigade Reserve NEW PARADE, NIEUPORT	—

A. Kyle Lieutenant
Commanding 18th Highland Light Infantry

Confidential.

WK 23

22. P.
6 sheets

War Diary
of the
16th Bn Highland Light Infantry
Volume XXIV

from 1st to 31st October 1917.

Army Form C. 2118.

WAR DIARY
or
INTELLIGENCE SUMMARY
(Erase heading not required.)

Volume XXII   Page 1.

Instructions regarding War Diaries and Intelligence Summaries are contained in F. S. Regs., Part II. and the Staff Manual respectively. Title Pages will be prepared in manuscript.

Place	Date 1917 October	Hour	Summary of Events and Information	Remarks and references to Appendices
NIEUPORT	1st		In Brigade Reserve in NEW PARADE, NIEUPORT. Information was received that the Military Cross has been awarded to 2nd Lieut John McClellan for conspicuous Gallantry in going to the assistance of a British aeroplane which had been shot down, and was lying in the middle of "No Man's Land" in front of the Belgian lines near RAMSCAPPELLE. Lieut McClellan went out with two Belgian soldiers who returned to their own lines when the enemy opened fire with M.G's in the vicinity of the plane. Lieut McClellan went on alone under heavy shell fire, ascertained that both pilot and observer were killed, and salvaged the maps, and other lose property. Casualties: Wounded 3 O.R.	w/f
NIEUPORT	2nd		In Brigade Reserve in NEW PARADE, NIEUPORT. The Battalion relieved the 2nd Bn K.O.Y.L.I. in the Lombardzyde Right Subsector relief complete 11.30pm. Casualties: Killed 1 O.R. Wounded 8 O.R.	w/f
LOMBARDZYDE Right Subsector	3rd		In occupation of LOMBARDZYDE Right Subsector. Casualties: Wounded 5 O.R. Reinforcements of 5 O.R. joined the Battalion on this date	w/f

Army Form C. 2118.

WAR DIARY
or
INTELLIGENCE SUMMARY

Volume XXIV Page 2

(Erase heading not required.)

Instructions regarding War Diaries and Intelligence Summaries are contained in F. S. Regs., Part II. and the Staff Manual respectively. Title Pages will be prepared in manuscript.

Place	Date	Hour	Summary of Events and Information	Remarks and references to Appendices
LOMBARDZYDE Right Subsector	4th		In occupation of LOMBARDZYDE Right Subsector. Casualties:- Wounded 5 o.r.	w.e/t
Do	5th		In occupation of LOMBARDZYDE Right Subsector. The Battalion was relieved by the 5th Bn Lancashire Fusiliers and proceeded to Billets in COXYDE. Casualties: Wounded 2 o.r. Relief complete 11.30 p.m.	w.e/t
COXYDE	6th	12 noon	The Battalion proceeded by march route to ADINKERKE	w.e/t
		2.30 pm	The Battalion embarked on Barges at ADINKERKE, and proceeded from there to CHAPEAU ROUGE on the NIEUPORT- DUNKERQUE CANAL	
		8 pm	On arrival at CHAPEAU ROUGE the Battalion disembarked, and proceeded to Billets in TETEGHEM	
TETEGHEM	7th		In Billets TETEGHEM. Reinforcements of 4 o.r. joined Battalion on this date.	w.e/t
do	8th		In Billets TETEGHEM.	w.e/t
do.	9th		In Billets TETEGHEM. Reinforcements of 31 o.r. joined Battalion on this date	w.e/t

Army Form C. 2118.

Volume XXIV Page 3.

WAR DIARY
or
INTELLIGENCE SUMMARY

(Erase heading not required.)

Instructions regarding War Diaries and Intelligence Summaries are contained in F. S. Regs., Part II. and the Staff Manual respectively. Title Pages will be prepared in manuscript.

Place	Date	Hour	Summary of Events and Information	Remarks and references to Appendices
TETEGHEM	10th		In Billets in TETEGHEM	will
Do	11th		In Billets in TETEGHEM	will
Do	12th		In Billets in TETEGHEM	will
Do	13th		In Billets in TETEGHEM	will
Do	14th		In Billets in TETEGHEM. The following Officers joined the Battalion on this date:— 2nd Lieut R.B. Robinson from 6th A.L.I. 2nd Lieut D. McNeal do.	well
Do	15th		In Billets in TETEGHEM. The following Officer joined Battalion on this date:— Captain J.J. Craven from 3rd A.L.I.	well
Do	16th		In Billets in TETEGHEM	well
Do	17th		In Billets in TETEGHEM	well

2449 Wt. W14957/M90 750,000 1/16 J.B.C. & A. Forms/C.2118/12.

Army Form C. 2118.

WAR DIARY
or
INTELLIGENCE SUMMARY

Volume XXIV page 4

Place	Date	Hour	Summary of Events and Information	Remarks and references to Appendices
TETEGHEM.	18th		In Billets in TETEGHEM.	w.e.f.
Do	19th		In Billets in TETEGHEM. A Regimental Concert was held in the Aerodrome by kind permission of Officer Commanding 24th Squadron R.F.C.	w.e.f.
Do	20th		In Billets in TETEGHEM	w.e.f.
Do	21st		In Billets in TETEGHEM. Reinforcements of 4 o.r. joined Battalion	w.e.f.
Do	22nd		In Billets in TETEGHEM. Reinforcements of 5 o.r. joined Battalion	w.e.f.
Do	23rd		In Billets in TETEGHEM. Lieut.Colonel R. Kerr assumed Command of 97th Brigade during the temporary absence of the Brigadier General. 32nd Division. Major H.S. Scott D.S.O., M.G. assumes Command of the Battalion	w.e.f.
Do	24th		In Billets in TETEGHEM. The Battalion moved by march route to Billets in ERINGHEM	w.e.f.

Army Form C. 2118.

WAR DIARY
or
INTELLIGENCE SUMMARY

(Erase heading not required.)

Volume XXIV Page 5.

Instructions regarding War Diaries and Intelligence Summaries are contained in F. S. Regs., Part II. and the Staff Manual respectively. Title Pages will be prepared in manuscript.

Place	Date	Hour	Summary of Events and Information	Remarks and references to Appendices
ERINGHEM	25th		In Billets in ERINGHEM.	wef
BROXEELE	26th		The Battalion moved from ERINGHEM to Billets in BROXEELE. Lieut Colonel R.Nyfe reassumed Command of the Battalion.	wef
Do	27th		In Billets in BROXEELE	wef
Do	28th		In Billets in BROXEELE	wef
Do	29th		In Billets in BROXEELE	wef
Do	30th		In Billets in BROXEELE	wef
Do	31st		In Billets in BROXEELE	wef

R.Nyfe Lieut-Colonel,
Commanding, 16th Highland Light Infantry

Vol 24

23.P.
6 sheets

War Diary
of the
16th Battalion Highland Light Infantry

Volume XXV

1st to 30th Nov. 1917.

Volume 25 Page 1

Army Form C. 2118.

WAR DIARY
or
INTELLIGENCE SUMMARY.
(Erase heading not required.)

Instructions regarding War Diaries and Intelligence Summaries are contained in F. S. Regs., Part II. and the Staff Manual respectively. Title pages will be prepared in manuscript.

Place	Date 1917 Nov.	Hour	Summary of Events and Information	Remarks and references to Appendices
BROXEELE	1st		In Billets in BROXEELE	nil
do.	2nd		In Billets in BROXEELE	nil
do.	3rd		In Billets in BROXEELE	nil
do.	4th		In Billets in BROXEELE	nil
do.	5th		In Billets in BROXEELE	nil
do.	6th		In Billets in BROXEELE	nil
do.	7th		In Billets in BROXEELE	nil

WAR DIARY or INTELLIGENCE SUMMARY

Volume 25 Page 2

Army Form C. 2118.

Place	Date 1917 Nov.	Hour	Summary of Events and Information	Remarks and references to Appendices
BROXEELE	8th		In Billets BROXEELE	nil
do.	9th		In Billets BROXEELE	nil
do.	10th		In Billets BROXEELE. The Battalion moved from Billets in BROXEELE to encampment at J.7.a.3.3 sheet 27.	nil
Camp at J.7.a.3.3	11th		In Camp at J.7.a.3.3. sheet 27. The Battalion moved to hutments in ROAD CAMP	nil
ROAD CAMP	12th		In hutments in ROAD CAMP. VAN DER BIEZEN	nil
do.	13th		In hutments in ROAD CAMP	nil

Army Form C. 2118.

WAR DIARY
or
INTELLIGENCE SUMMARY.
(Erase heading not required.)

Volume 25 Page 3

Instructions regarding War Diaries and Intelligence Summaries are contained in F. S. Regs., Part II. and the Staff Manual respectively. Title pages will be prepared in manuscript.

Place	Date 1917 NOV.	Hour	Summary of Events and Information	Remarks and references to Appendices
ROAD CAMP	14th		In hutments in ROAD CAMP. 3 or. reinforcements arrived this date	nil
Do	15th		In hutments in ROAD CAMP	nil
Do	16th		In hutments in ROAD CAMP. Reinforcements of 27 or. arrived this date	nil
Do	17th		In hutments in ROAD CAMP	nil
Do	18th		In hutments in ROAD CAMP	nil
Do	19th		In hutments in ROAD CAMP	nil

WAR DIARY
or
INTELLIGENCE SUMMARY.

(Erase heading not required.)

Volume 25 Page 4

Army Form C. 2118.

Place	Date 1917 Nov.	Hour	Summary of Events and Information	Remarks and references to Appendices
ROAD CAMP	20th		In hutments in ROAD CAMP	nil
Do	21/st		In hutments in ROAD CAMP	nil
Do	22nd		In hutments in ROAD CAMP. The Battalion moved by rail to IRISH FARM CAMP in C.27.a Sheet 28	nil
IRISH FARM	23rd		In IRISH FARM CAMP. The Battalion moved from IRISH CAMP to WURST FARM in D.7.B Sheet 28	nil
WURST FARM	24th		In WURST FARM.	nil
WURST FARM	25th		In WURST FARM. The Battalion relieved the 2nd K.O.Y.L.I. in the PASSCHENDAELE SECTOR. Left Division Right Brigade, 2nd Bn Scottish Rifles on right and 11th Border Regt on left. Relief complete at 10pm. The Battalion had the following casualties during the relief:-	nil

Volume 25 Page 5

WAR DIARY
or
INTELLIGENCE SUMMARY.
(Erase heading not required.)

Army Form C. 2118.

Place	Date	Hour	Summary of Events and Information	Remarks and references to Appendices
PASSCHENDAELE SECTOR (contd)	25th		Casualties Wounded in Action Captain E.A. McLELLAN 2nd Lieut W. COMRIE 2nd Lieut G.G. LEAH 2nd Lieut E.T. HILLIER Other ranks Killed 13 Wounded 39	
Do	26th		PASSCHENDAEL SECTOR The enemy put down his S.O.S. Barrage on this night and the following casualties were taken:- Killed Wounded Other ranks 10 23	
Do	27th		PASSCHENDAEL SECTOR Bn was relieved by 2nd Inniskilling Fusiliers and proceeded to Camp at WURST FARM. Relief complete 10 pm Casualties Killed Wounded Missing Other ranks 5 18 12	
FARM WURST CAMP	28th		In occupation of WURST CAMP The Bn moved to IRISH CAMP arriving there 2:30 pm Casualties 6 or Wounded	
IRISH FARM	29th		In occupation of IRISH FARM CAMP. Casualties 2 or Killed 2 or Wounded	
Do	30th		In occupation of IRISH FARM CAMP. The Battalion moved from IRISH CAMP to BELLEVUE completely equipped in Battle Order.	

Wm D. Scott
Major
Commanding 16th Highland Light Infantry

WO 25 97/37

2H.P.
23 sheets

War Diary
of the
16th Highland Light Infantry

Volume XXVI

1st to 31st December 1917.

2H.P.
23 sheets

Note: AREAS SHEWN WET ARE NOT NECESSARILY IMPASSABLE.
Shelter
M.G. (Approx. Position)
Post
3 M.G.s
Occupied
Concertina Wire
Pill Boxes intact
Occupied shell holes
Tall tree used as an O.P.
Consolidated shell holes
M.G. Post
M.G.s reported here
This trench appears to be in fair condition
Occupied shellhole
Wireless set
Telephone
M.G. unloaded here and carried to positions
M.G. Limbers
Rgtl H.Q.
This trench is in good cond.
Shelters
H.Q. Suspt in this small dugout
This Pill Box is intact
Intact
This dugout had a direct hit and is apparently destroyed
This dugout is used as a dressing stn
Strong Point
Reported strongly held
Unoccupied
Still intact
Post
M.G.
Dry
No 3 Coy
No 4 Coy
No 3 Coy
Tunnelled dugout
No 1 Coy
No 2 Coy
No 1 Coy
No 3 Coy
K.O.Y.L.I.
11th BORDER
16th H.L.I.
FORMING UP LINE
DUGOUTS OR SHELTERS
M.G.s REPORTED FIRING
OCCUPIED SHELL-HOLES
FLOODED AREAS
WET GROUND

Army Form C. 2118.

Volume XXVI Page 1

WAR DIARY
or
INTELLIGENCE SUMMARY.
(Erase heading not required.)

Instructions regarding War Diaries and Intelligence Summaries are contained in F. S. Regs., Part II. and the Staff Manual respectively. Title pages will be prepared in manuscript.

Place	Date	Hour	Summary of Events and Information	Remarks and references to Appendices
BELLEVUE	1917 Dec.	1pm	1. The Battalion occupied the trenches in vicinity of BELLEVUE (D.4.d. 50.45) in readiness to carry out the operation on PASSCHENDAEL RIDGE described in O.O. 16/3 (see appendix I) Strength 16 Officers and 404 O.T. At 5.30pm reinforcements were received of 4 Officers and 65 O.T. Total strength on going into action 20 Officers 469 O.T. (See appendix II). During daylight the Battalion was at rest. In spite of frequent bursts of hostile shell fire no casualties were taken. 2. At 6.30pm the taping party (Lieut. J. MACLELLAN, M.G., and 16 O.T.) moved off and laid a tape from D.6.a.0.6 near MOSSEMARKT, to front line position via VENTURE FARM. They then taped the assembly position and erected luminous numbered tins to mark the right of each platoon. The tape was laid on a Battalion frontage of 300 yds (see sketch map attached) and within a depth of 30 yds no experience had shown that this position was formed of the enemy's S.O.S. Barrage lines. 3. At 9.30pm the Battalion moved from BELLEVUE to the assembly position (Order of march - D, B, C, A Coys) and was in position at 11.10pm. Five casualties were taken from enemy shell fire during this move. 4. The Battalion was then in line with the 11th Borders on its left. The 2nd Div. L.I. had taken up a position on a parallel line to our right	

Volume XXV Page 2

WAR DIARY
or
INTELLIGENCE SUMMARY.

Army Form C. 2118.

Place	Date	Hour	Summary of Events and Information	Remarks and references to Appendices
BATTLE POSITION	1917 Aug.	10.30pm	5. At 10.30pm Advanced Battalion Headquarters under Lieut S.M. ROBERTS (Signalling Officer) were established at VIRILE FARM (V.29.b.70.45) and connected by wire with Battalion Headquarters at BELLEVUE.	
			6. Weather: bright moonlight, no wind, visibility good up to 300 yds. ground soft but quite practicable.	
Do	2nd		At Zero hour (1.55 am) the Battalion advanced. It was at once met with intense enemy machine gun fire from direction of MALLET COPSE, VOX FARM, VOID FARM, and "HILL 52". The enemy pill box and trenches at VOX FARM were at once rushed and the garrison disposed of. 50 prisoners being sent to the rear. Two enemy machine guns were captured here and afterwards sent to D.A.D.O.S.	
			The concentrated M.G. fire had severely thinned our ranks, and this fire was not checked until our barrage was put down at 2.3 am	
			8. The advance was then continued and at 2.40 am a long running E and W through VOID FARM (V.23.d.9.3) was reached. By this time touch had been lost with the unit on our left. Captains G.L. DAVIDSON and 2nd Lieut W.R. BEHMIE, were killed about this time by enemy sniper from direction of MALLET COPSE, whilst endeavouring to locate this unit.	

Army Form C. 2118.

Volume XXVI Page 3.

WAR DIARY
or
INTELLIGENCE SUMMARY.
(Erase heading not required.)

Instructions regarding War Diaries and Intelligence Summaries are contained in F. S. Regs., Part II. and the Staff Manual respectively. Title pages will be prepared in manuscript.

Place	Date	Hour	Summary of Events and Information	Remarks and references to Appendices
BATTLE POSITION	1917 Dec. 2nd.		The wind on our right had been caught in the enemy barrage and were unable to get forward, so that our right flank was exposed.	any
			9. The remnants of the Battalion then consolidated two positions on the line of our first objective. One under Lieut. J. MILLER and Lieut. J.W. LUNN with about 40 o.r. from B and D Companies, was immediately in front of VOID FARM about V.23.a.9.4. facing N. The other under Captain J. ALEXANDER, Lieut. D.V. CHARLTON and Lieut. R.I.B ROBERTSON, with about 30 o.r. from A & C Companies was about V.24.c.3.4. facing N.E. These positions were held until orders to withdraw were received at 5 am on 3rd December, 1917.	
			10. During daylight 2nd December 1917, Enemy aeroplanes were very active, flying low over our positions, but there was little enemy artillery activity.	
			11. About 4pm the enemy infantry were observed to be concentrating on the N. side of MALLET COPSE and about V.24. central. Our S.O.S. was fired by Lieut. CHARLTON, and our barrage was promptly put down. The enemy infantry attacked our positions about 4.30pm, but were driven off by Lewis Gun and rifle fire, with the assistance of one Vickers gun which had been brought up.	
			12. During this operation Captain ALEXANDER was found to be Missing. It is believed that he was caught by a shell while visiting the shell hole posts.	

Army Form C. 2118.

WAR DIARY
or
INTELLIGENCE SUMMARY.
(Erase heading not required.)

VOLUME XXVI Page 4

Instructions regarding War Diaries and Intelligence Summaries are contained in F. S. Regs. Part II. and the Staff Manual respectively. Title pages will be prepared in manuscript.

Place	Date	Hour	Summary of Events and Information	Remarks and references to Appendices
BATTLE POSITION	1917 Dec 2nd		13. About 4.15 p.m. during the enemy bombardment, a shell entered Battalion Headquarters on the BELLEVUE PILL BOX, killing Lieut. J. FERRIS (attached T.M.B.), the artillery Liaison Officer and J.O., and wounding Major W. D. SCOTT, D.S.O., M.C., who was in command, Lieut. J. McLELLAM, M.C., another T.M.B. Officer and 3 O.R. At 7.30 p.m. Major SCOTT reported at Brigade Headquarters and Command of the Battalion was transferred to O.C. 15th Northumberland Fusiliers the Battalion in support. Casualties :- Killed in Action Captain G.L. DAVIDSON 2/Lieut W.R. BEMHIE 2/Lieut J. WHITFIELD 2/Lieut J. FERRIS 19 Other Ranks. Wounded in Action Major W.D. SCOTT D.S.O.,M.C. Lieut C.W. DURWARD Lieut D. DEWAR 2/Lieut S.M. MURRAY 2/Lieut A. ELDER 2/Lieut R.G.A. TEMPLE 2/Lieut G.B. GRANT (Died of Wounds) 2/Lieut H.V. JOWETT 2/Lieut J. McLELLAM, M.C. 179 Other Ranks.	

WAR DIARY or INTELLIGENCE SUMMARY

VOLUME XXVI Page 5.

Army Form C. 2118.

Place	Date	Hour	Summary of Events and Information	Remarks and references to Appendices
BATTLE POSITION	1917 Dec 2nd		Casualties (Continued) Wounded and Missing 4 Other ranks Captain J. ALEXANDER (believed killed) Missing 41 Other ranks	
Do.	3rd	4. 5 am	O.C. 16th Northumberland Fusiliers ordered the Battalion to withdraw to a position about V.29.B.3.4. N.W. of VIRILE FARM. This position was completed without casualties by 6 am	
		15.	The Battalion held this position throughout the day and was relieved by the 5/6th Royal Scots and 1st Dorsets during the night 3/4th December.	
Do.	4th		This relief was completed by 3 am when the Battalion moved to IRISH FARM and there entrained at 9 am for BRAKE CAMP, arriving there at 11 am. Captain A. FRASER in command. Strength on arriving out of action was 8 Officers 204 other ranks.	
BRAKE CAMP	5th		G. Antmark. BRAKE CAMP	

Volume XXVI Page 6

WAR DIARY
or
INTELLIGENCE SUMMARY.

(Erase heading not required.)

Army Form C. 2118.

Place	Date 1917 September	Hour	Summary of Events and Information	Remarks and references to Appendices
BRAKE CAMP	6th		In Hutments BRAKE CAMP	—
Do	7th		In Hutments BRAKE CAMP. The Battalion moved by rail from BRAKE CAMP to Camp at IRISH FARM	—
IRISH FARM	8th		In Camp at IRISH FARM	—
Do	9th		In Camp at IRISH FARM	—
Do	10th		In Camp at IRISH FARM	—
Do	11th		In Camp at IRISH FARM. 1 O.R. Wounded	—
Do	12th		In Camp at IRISH CAMP. 3 O.R. Wounded	—

Army Form C. 2118.

WAR DIARY
or
INTELLIGENCE SUMMARY.
(Erase heading not required.)

Volume XXVI Page 7

Instructions regarding War Diaries and Intelligence Summaries are contained in F. S. Regs., Part II. and the Staff Manual respectively. Title pages will be prepared in manuscript.

Place	Date	Hour	Summary of Events and Information	Remarks and references to Appendices
IRISH FARM	13th		In Camp at IRISH FARM	nil
Do	14th		In Camp at IRISH FARM	nil
Do	15th		In Camp at IRISH FARM	nil
Do	16th		In Camp at IRISH FARM. Reinforcement of 3 o.r. joined Battalion on this date	nil
Do	17th		In Camp at IRISH FARM. The Battalion moved from IRISH FARM to Brigade Reserve in HILLTOP FARM.	nil
HILLTOP FARM	18th		In Brigade Reserve at HILLTOP FARM	nil
Do	19th		In Brigade Reserve at HILLTOP FARM. Reinforcement of 33 o.r. joined Battalion on this date	nil
Do	20th		In Brigade Reserve at HILLTOP FARM.	nil

A5634 Wt. W4973 M687 750,000 8/16 D. D. & L. Ltd. Forms/C.2118/13.

Volume XXVI Page 8.

Army Form C. 2118.

WAR DIARY
or
INTELLIGENCE SUMMARY.

(Erase heading not required.)

Instructions regarding War Diaries and Intelligence Summaries are contained in F. S. Regs., Part II. and the Staff Manual respectively. Title pages will be prepared in manuscript.

Place	Date	Hour	Summary of Events and Information	Remarks and references to Appendices
HILLTOP FARM	20th		The Battalion moved from HILLTOP FARM, and relieved the 2nd K.O.Y.L.I. in the Left Subsector of — Relief complete 10.30pm.	
LEFT SUBSECTOR	21st		In occupation of Left Sub-sector. 2 O.R. wounded	
Do	22nd		In occupation of Left Subsector. 1 O.R. wounded.	
Do	23rd		In occupation of Left Subsector. The Bn was relieved by the 1st Dorset Regiment and proceeded by rail to hutments in SIEGE CAMP. Relief complete 8.30pm	
SIEGE CAMP	24th		In hutments SIEGE CAMP	
SIEGE CAMP	25th		In hutments SIEGE CAMP	
Do	26th		In hutments SIEGE CAMP	

Volume XXVI Page 9

WAR DIARY
INTELLIGENCE SUMMARY.

Army Form C. 2118.

Place	Date	Hour	Summary of Events and Information	Remarks and references to Appendices
SIEGE CAMP	27th		In huttments SIEGE CAMP	
Do	28th		In huttments SIEGE CAMP. By authority granted by His Majesty the King the Field Marshal Commanding-in-chief has awarded the following decoration Distinguished Service Order — Capt. F. CARR HARRIS RAMC attached 13th H.L.I.	
Do	29th		In huttments SIEGE CAMP	
Do	30th		In huttments SIEGE CAMP. The Battalion moved from SIEGE CAMP by rail to Billets in LOUCHES	
LOUCHES	31st		In Billets in LOUCHES.	

Wm D. Scott
Major
Commanding 13th Highrs L.I.

APPENDIX II.

List of Officers who went into action
with the Battalion on 1/2nd December, 1917.

Major W.D. Scott, D.S.O. M.C.
Captain A. Fraser
2/Lieut J. McLellan, M.C.
2/Lieut S.M. Roberts

2/Lieut S.M. Murray
2/Lieut R.G.A. Temple
2/Lieut H.V. Jowett
2/Lieut A. Elder

Captain G.L. Davidson
2/Lieut J. Miller
2/Lieut W.R. Bennie
Lieut J.W. Lunn

Captain J. Alexander
2/Lieut H.H. Edie.
2/Lieut J. Whitfield
2/Lieut R.B. Robertson

Lieut D. Dewar
2/Lieut D.V. Charlton
2/Lieut C.B. Grant
Lieut C.W. Durward

Captain F.F. Carr Harris   Medical Officer

Ref. A.O.1.

To : Officers Commanding,

All Companies.

1. The date of "Y" day is 1st December.
The attack will therefore take place on the night of 1/2nd December.
The hour of zero will be 1.55 a.m. on the morning of 2nd December, 1917.

2. The Battalion will move to the assembly position and will pass the starting point D.5.c.1.5. at 9.25 p.m.
The Battalion should be clear of the BELLEVUE Cross Roads by 10.10 p.m.

3. The order of march will be as follows :-
D, C, B, A Companies

4. A hot meal of tea and rum will be carried up and issued to the Battalion at 5.30 p.m.

5. A taping party of 4 N.C.O's per company and Cpl HILLEY and Cpl GILMOUR will report to Lieut McLELLAN at Battalion Headquarters at 6.30 p.m. A guide from Battalion H.Q., will guide the Battalion up to the position of assembly position where the tape leaves the MOSSELMARKT Road.

6. O.C. B Company will detail 2 guides to meet the detachment of Machine Guns who are attached to the Battalion The guides should be at BELLEVUE - point D.4.d.7.2. and meet the M.G's there after PRINT has passed on.

7. Battalion Advanced Headquarters will be at VOCATION FARM All messages and reports will be sent there.

8. Reference last line of para. 10 (Action of Artillery) for 200 yards substitute 300 yards.

Macfarlay
Captain and Adjutant,
16th Highland Light Infantry

1st December, 1917.

ref. 16/6.

16th Highland Light Infantry

(No. 2. Battalion)

OPERATION ORDERS

G. Davidson.
OC. "B" Co.

1. GENERAL SCHEME OF ATTACK

(a) The 2nd Corps will continue operations on a date to be notified later with the object of driving the enemy from the PASSCHENDAEL RIDGE. The 8th Corps will operate on the right of the 2nd Corps.

(b) The first phase of the operations will be the capture of the RED line (vide attached map 'A')

(c) The attack will be carried out at night.

2. ACTION OF THE 92th INFANTRY BRIGADE

The attack and capture of the RED line on the 2nd Corps front has been entrusted to the 97th Infantry Brigade with one Battalion (15th Lancs Fusrs) of the 96th Infantry Brigade attached.

The 16th North. Fus. (96th Brigade) will be attached to the 97th Infantry Brigade for the attack and will be used as Counter-Counter-attacking troops.

These two Battalions will be holding the line on the night of the attack and will come under the orders of G.O.C., 97th Infantry Brigade on Y/Z night at an hour to be notified later.

3. DATE AND HOUR OF ATTACK

The attack will be carried out on Y/Z night. The date of Y day and the hour of ZERO will be notified later.

4. OBJECTIVES AND BOUNDARIES

Objectives and Boundaries are shown on the attached map 'A'

5. ASSEMBLY

At ZERO hour on Y/Z night Battalions will be assembled on a taped line as shown in the attached map.

Orders regarding the laying of the tapes and the march to the assembly will be issued separately.

6. FORMATION AND FRONTAGES

(a) The Brigade will assemble on a frontage of 1850 yards with five Battalions in line as under :-

```
No. 1. Battalion.  - 2nd K.O.Y.L.I.   frontage 400 yards
No. 2.     ..      - 16th High. L. I. frontage 300 yards
No. 3.     ..      - 11th Border R.      ..    300 yards
No. 4.     ..      - 17th High. L. I.    ..    400 yards
No. 5.     ..      - 15th Lancs Fus.     ..    450 yards
```

The frontage of Battalions on their final objective will be as follows :-

```
No. 1. Battalion 520 yards
No. 2.     ..    450  ..
No. 3.     ..    400  ..
No. 4.     ..    500  ..
No. 5      ..    700  ..
```

6. FORMATION AND FRONTAGES Contd.

No. 6 Battalion (16th North Fus.) will be holding the Right Subsector of the Brigade line on Y day and will commence to assemble on Y/Z night in the neighbourhood of VIRILE FARM at ZERO plus 1½ hours.

(b) Nos 1. and 5. Battalions will attack on a three Company frontage with one Company in Support, moving in rear on No.2 Company.
Nos 2, 3, and 4 Battalions will attack on a two Company frontage with Nos 3 and 4 Coys in rear of Nos 1 and 2 Companies respectively.
The 16th High. L. I. companies will be as follows :-
    No.1. Company   -   "C" Company
    No.2.   ..   -   "D"   ..
    No.3.   ..   -   "A"   ..
    No.4.   ..   -   "B"   ..

(c) All Companies will be assembled on a two platoon frontage forming four waves as follows :-
    First Wave : 3 sections of each of Nos 1 and 2 platoons in line of sections in snake formation (i.e. not extended)
    Second Wave : Lewis Gun Sections and platoon Headquarters of Nos 1 and 2 platoons in snake formation.
    Third Wave : 3 sections of each of Nos 3 and 4 platoons similar to First Wave.
    Fourth Wave : Lewis Gun sections and platoon Headquarters of Nos 3 and 4 Platoons in snake formation.

Distances between waves - 20 yards
Distances between Companies - 40 yards.

7. METHOD OF ATTACK

General method of attack
(1) Definite and distinct units will be detailed to capture, garrison and consolidate definite objectives and areas.
(2) The essence of the attack is surprise.
There will therefore be no increase of artillery fire until ZERO plus 8 minutes by which time it is estimated that the alarm will have been given by the enemy.
The subsequent action of the artillery is given in para 9.

Action of attacking Battalions
(1) No.1. Battalion
    (a) Nos 1 2 and 3 Coys will advance straight to the final objective on the RED line. These Coys will be responsible for the capture of all localities and Strong points occupied by the enemy between our assembly positions and the final objective.
    (b) No. 4. Company will move forward in rear of No.2 Company and will be prepared to :-
        (i) Support any of the leading Coys should it become necessary to do so to enable these Coys to reach their final objectives.
        (ii) Give assistance to the left Battalion of the Brigade on our right in the event of its being held up by forming a defensive flank facing East.
        Should neither of the above eventualities occur No.4 Coy will consolidate in depth in the area shown in Map 'A'.
        The denial of Hill 52 to the enemy is essential to the success of the operations.
(2) Nos 2, 3, and 4 Battalions.
    (a) Nos 1 and 2 Coys will advance as far as dotted GREEN line marked on the map and will be responsible for the capture of all occupied localities between the assemby positions and the dotted GREEN line

(2) Continued.
(b) Nos 3 and 4 Coys will follow Nos 1 and 2 Coys, leap-frog on the dotted GREEN line and advance to the final objective and will be responsible for the capture of all occupied localities between the dotted GREEN line and their final objective.

Action of 16th High. L. I.

No. 1. Company (C Coy) will attack on a two platoon frontage, 9 and 10 platoons leading, supported by 11 and 12 platoons. Nos 9, 10, and 12 platoons will consolidate on the GREEN line objective. No. 11 will be in close support at Company Headquarters.

No. 2. Company (D Coy) will attack on a two platoon frontage, Nos 13 and 14 platoons leading supported by Nos 15 and 16 Platoons respectively. No. 14 platoon will capture and consolidate VOID FARM. Nos 13, 15, and 16 Platoons will consolidate on the GREEN line objective.

No. 3. Company (A Coy) will attack on a two platoon frontage, Nos 2 and 4 platoons leading supported by Nos 1 and 3. Nos 1, 2, and 4, will consolidate on the final objective (RED LINE) with No.3 platoon in close support at Company Headquarters.

No. 4 Company (B Coy) will attack on a two platoon frontage, 6 and 8 platoons leading, supported by 5 and 7 platoons. No. 6 platoon will capture and consolidate VOLT FARM and will be in support there at Company Headquarters. 5, 7, and 8 platoons will consolidate on the final objective (RED LINE)

(3) No. 5. Battalion -
(a) Nos 1, 2, and 3 Coys will advance to the RED line and thus form a defensive flank entirely from the left of the present front line to the left of No.4. Battalion on their final objective.
(b) No.4. Coy will move forward in rear of No.1. Coy and will be prepared to support any of the leading Coys should it become necessary to do so to enable these Coys to reach their final objectives.
Should this not be required No.4 Coy will consolidate in depth in the area marked on the map.

8. ACTION OF COUNTER-COUNTER ATTACKING TROOPS

No.6. Battalion will commence to assemble in the vicinity of VIRILE FARM at ZERO plus 1½ hours and will be prepared to move forward to re-establish our final objective in the event of a heavy hostile Counter attack developing on the Brigade front.

The responsibility for moving forward will rest with the O.C. No.6. Battalion who will keep himself informed of the situation.

9. ACTION OF ARTILLERY

From ZERO to ZERO plus 8 minutes artillery fire will be normal.
At ZERO plus 8 minutes artillery will open fire on selected points within the area to be attacked and NORTH of a line drawn 350 yards to the North of and parallel to the taped line of assembly.
At ZERO plus 14 minutes artillery will lift off all points to the North of this line but South of a similar line drawn 450 yards to the North of and parallel to taped line of assembly.
At ZERO plus 20 minutes artillery will lift off all points South of a similar line 550 yards from the taped line of assembly.
At ZERO plus 26 minutes artillery will lift off all points South of a similar line 650 yards from taped line of assembly.
At ZERO plus 32 minutes artillery will lift off all points South of a similar line 750 yards from taped line of assembly.
As artillery reaches the objective it will form a protective barrage 200 yards clear of the RED LINE.

10. CONSOLIDATION

(a) Final Objective, Front line

The RED line will be strongly consolidated by troops detailed below.

Method - Short lengths of trench forming mutually supporting posts, accommodating a section.

The line will be carefully sited by Company Commanders concerned.

(b) Support line

A Support line will be formed by troops detailed below along vicinity of the dotted GREEN Line.

Method - Lengths of trench to accommodate a platoon.

(c) Strong points

Will be constructed as follows :-
- No.1.   Hill 52
- No.2   VOLT FME
- No.3.   VOID FARM
- No.4.   MALLET COPSE
- No.5.   VEAL COTTAGES
- No.6.   ENCLOSURES at V.22.d.9.2.

(d) Troops allotted

No.1. Battalion
- No.1. Company — 3 platoons front line - 1 platoon close support to front line.
- No.2. Company — -do-
- No.3. Company — -do-
- No.4. Company — 2 platoons support line about V.30.a.7.8. 2 platoons Strong point Hill 52.

No. 2. Battalion
- No.1. Company — Support line within its area.
- No.2. Company — Support line within its area including VOID FARM Strong point.
- No.3. Company — 3 platoons front line, 1 platoon in close support to front line.
- No. 4. Company — 3 platoons in front line, 1 platoon in close support in VOLT FME Strong point.

No.3. Battalion
- No.1. Company — Support line in area.
- No.2. Company — -do-
- No.3. Company — 3 platoons front line. 1 platoon in close support to front line.
- No.4. Company — 2 Platoons in front line, 2 platoons MALLET COPSE Strong point.

No.4. Battalion
- No.1. Company — Support line within its area, including VEAL COTTAGES Strong point.
- No.2. Company — Support line within its area.
- No.3. Company — 3 Platoons front line. 1 platoon in close support to front line.
- No.4. Company — -do-

No.5. Battalion
- No.1. Company — 3 platoons front line, 1 platoon in Strong point in V.22.d.9.2.
- No.2. Company — 3 platoons front line, 1 platoon in close support to front line.
- No.3. Company — will hold its original position with two left platoons, 2 right platoons front line.
- No.4. Company — Support line about V.29.a.1.6.

11. ACTION OF R.E.

(1) (a) The O.C. 219th Field Company R.E. will detail two parties each consisting of 1 Subaltern and 4 Sappers to superintend the construction of the Strong points on Hill 52 and VOID FARM.

They will assemble and move forward as follows :-
Hill 52 party with No.4 Company of No.1. Battalion.
VOID FARM party with No.2. Company of No.2. Battalion.

(b) The role of these parties will be to assist the Company Commander in the construction of these Strong points while the latter are organising the defence of their line.

(2) The remainder of the 219th Field Company R.E. with 100 attached Infantry will be under the orders of the O.C. Coy who will be responsible for the maintenance of the forward portion of MOUSETRAP and No.6. Tracks and the continuation of these tracks forward.

12 MACHINE GUNS

The O.C. 97th M.G. Coy will allot Machine Guns to positions shown in map sent him.

Sub sections with their carrying parties of attached Infantry will assemble with, and move forward in rear of, the Coys to whose area they are allotted.

In addition to the close defence guns, machine guns will be organised into -
(a) Barrage guns
(b) Area concentration Guns
) under the orders of the Corps
) M.G. Officer

(i) Barrage guns
10 Batteries will be allotted for this work.
The task of these guns will be :-
(a) To form a protective barrage in front of the Objective.
(b) To search and sweep the area within the limits of their range, where the enemy's reserves are known to be concentrated.

(ii) Area Concentration Guns
6 Batteries are allotted for this work until ZERO plus 1½ hours at which hour one battery will be withdrawn from area concentration fire and will advance to occupy positions in the captured area vide (iii) below.
The task of area concentration guns will be :-
(a) To maintain concentration of fire on areas where the enemy is likely to be assembling for a Counter attack or over which his Counter attacking troops will be likely to pass.
(b) To keep under fire the defensive localities not included in the Objective on the left flank of the attack where snipers and machine guns may be active.

(iii) One Battery allotted for area concentration fire will be withdrawn from this task at ZERO plus 1½ hours and will advance and occupy the following positions :-
½ Section - Strong point at Hill 52
½ section - Strong point at VOID FARM
½ section - Strong point at MALLET COPSE.
½ section - Strong point at VEAL COTTAGES.
These guns will come under the orders of the G.O.C. 97th Infantry Brigade at ZERO plus 1½ hours.

(iv) The Corps Machine Officer will be at the 32nd Divisional Headquarters and the Divisional Machine Gun Officer at 97th Infantry Brigade Headquarters from ZERO onwards.

13. LIGHT TRENCH MORTARS

(1) Dumps of L.T.M's ammunition will be established by Y/Z night at SOURCE FME and VENTURE FARM.
(2) At ZERO hour the 97th T.M. Battery less two guns will be assembled in the GOUDBERGH RAVINE in V.29.d.
The remaining two guns will assemble at SOURCE FME.
(3) At ZERO Plus 1½ hours teams will commence moving forward their guns and Dumps to the positions shown on map issued.
(4) In the case of a heavy Counter attack developing the trench Mortars will open rapid fire with all available ammunition. The guns will not be unmasked by firing at a small isolated Counter attack.

14. POSITION OF HEADQUARTERS.

Brigade Headquarters will be established at KRONPRINZ FARM with an advanced report centre at point 83 D.4.a.8.4.
The position of Battalion Headquarters will be as follows :-
No.1. Battalion - MEETSCHEELE - D.5.c.90.95.
No.2. Battalion - ~~VINE COTTAGE~~ ~~V.29.c.05.25.~~ BELLEVUE. D.Hd.7.2.
No.3. Battalion - BELLEVUE   - D.5.c.05.55.
No.4. Battalion)
No.5. Battalion) Point 83 D.4.a.8.4.
No.6. Battalion VIRILE FARM V.29.b.80.45.
The Battalion H.Q. of the left Battalion of the 8th Division will be at D.5.c.90.95. adjoining No.1. Battalion.

15. COMMUNICATIONS

WIRES The various Battalion Headquarters will be connected to Brigade by the following means :-
Laddered lines will be laid from KRONPRINZ FARM to point 83(D.4.a.8.4.) to Nos 4. and 5. Bns and continued forward via VINE COTT. (No2. Battalion) to VIRILE FARM where a Brigade Forward Station will be established.
From VINE COTT. to Battalion Headquarters at MEETCHEELE a laddered line will be laid.
The Battalion at BELLEVUE will have communication with the Brigade Via the buried system and a laddered line will be laid from the head of the bury at BELLEVUE to the Bn Headquarters at MEETCHEELE.
This provides telephonic communication between Headquarters of units.
Messages from the front can be sent by runner to any of the linesmen posts at VIRILE FARM, VINE COTT. and pt 83., whence they will be transmitted to Headquarters by any means possible.
In the event of a Battalion establishing a forward H.Q. the Battalion Signallers will lay and maintain a line to the nearest of the three linesmen's posts pt 83, VINE COTT., VIRILE FARM.

WIRELESS Wireless Stations will be established at following Infantry Headquarters and will be in communication with one another :-
  1. BELLEVUE
  2. KRONPRINZ
  3. KANSAS CROSS
Set 1 will also communicate with Rt Bde.
Except in cases of emergency messages will be sent in code and will be enciphered and deciphered by the WIRELESS OPERATORS unless franked "in clear" by an Officer.
In all cases messages must be brief.
Special attention is called to this means in case of S.O.S. messages and cancel S.O.S. messages.

15 COMMUNICATIONS Contd.

VISUAL This means should prove of great use and will be Thoroughly organised.

A Brigade central visual station will be established at BELLEVUE. This station will be in direct communication with Battalion Headquarters. Messages will be sent from front to rear only except between KRONPRINZ and BELLEVUE. Men will be told off from each Battalion.

Rate of sending will not exceed 8 words and messages will be sent twice.

Red lights will be used.

The visual station at BELLEVUE will be in direct communication by visual with KRONPRINZ.

Battalion Signalling Officers will organise their own visual communication and will ensure that Coys keep in communication by visual with selected stations.

Red lights will be used for all Infantry communications.

RUNNERS Runners Posts will be organised at a distance of 400 to 500 yards interval along a line from KRONPRINZ – VINE COTT. to VIRILE FARM.

Runners to Battalion at MEETCHEELE and BELLEVUE will work direct along No.6. track to PETER PAN and thence to BELLEVUE.

Battalion Signalling Officers will arrange forward runner relay posts in area of Battalion attack.

A total of 8 runners per Battalion will be required and these will report to Bde H.Q. at place and time to be notified later.

PIGEONS Each Battalion will be supplied with 8 pigeons. These should go forward with the attacking Coys. They must not be used before daylight.

AEROPLANES A Signal aeroplane will fly throughout Z day and will receive messages from any Battalion H.Q. Battalions wishing to send messages to Plane will call up with its own call to which the aeroplane will reply by repeating the call.

The message will then be sent, groups being answered by T.

Finally after V.E. the aeroplane will answer station call and R.D.

16 AEROPLANES

1. A contact aeroplane will fly over the line at 7.30 a.m. on the morning of the attack and will call for flares by sending a succession of A's on the KLAXON horn and dropping a white light.

   The most advanced line of Infantry will burn green flares at this hour as soon as called for by the aeroplane.

   Flares will not be burnt unless called for by the aeroplane.

2. The most advanced line of attacking infantry will also burn green ground flares at all other times when called for by contact aeroplanes in the manner indicated in para 1.

3. Infantry will at the same time as burning flares signal their position to the aeroplane by waving WATSON FANS.

4. All troops will be warned :-
   (a) That the contact aeroplanes are marked by two oblong black panels fixed at right angles to the rear edge of the lower plane, one on each side of the fusilage and about three feet from it.

8.

16. AEROPLANES Contd.

4 contd
(b) That flares are not to be lit if called for by an aeroplane which does not carry the markings described in (a) above.

5. An aeroplane will be in the air from dawn on the morning of the day of attack to watch for any indication of impending Counter attacks and to give warning of same by wireless and by dropping a WHITE PARACHUTE LIGHT.

6. Contact aeroplanes will drop messages at MXXXXX 32nd Divisional Headquarters, CANAL BANK, C.25.d..

17. MAINTENANCE OF DIRECTION

1. Every possible means and device for ensuring direction being kept is to be employed.
2. Every officer and as many N.C.O's as possible must be provided with compasses and know the compass bearing of their objective.
3. In the centre of each Company assembly position a luminous notice board will be put up on which is painted the bearing of the First Company objective and the distance in yards to it.

18. WATCHES.

Orders regarding the synchronisation of watches will be intimated in the orders for the assembly.

19. Stretcher Bearers, etc

Instructions regarding Prisoners of War, Medical arrangements, Stretcher Posts, etc, will be issued separately.

All Battalion Stretcher Bearers will assemble in trenches in the vicinity of VIRILE FARM and will clear the area after the Battalion has advanced.

20. ASSEMBLY PARTY

Lieut McLELLAN and one man per platoon will lay the tapes and place luminous Platoon boards in position. Each board will be placed on the RIGHT of each platoon frontage.

The hour at which this party will assemble will be intimated later..

21. REPORTS

O.C. Coys will forward to Battalion Headquarters as frequently as the situation permits reports as to the progress of the operations.

22. ADMINISTRATION.

Battle Stores will be carried in accordance with circulars issued on 19th November and marked 21 and 22.

Captain & Adjutant, for
Major, Commanding, 16th Highrs. L. I.

29th November, 1917.

SECRET

32nd Div.No.G.S.1357/7/2.

NOTES TO ACCOMPANY OPERATION ORDERS.

STRONG POINTS. 1. Definite distinct and complete units must be detailed to capture, mop up and garrison each known enemy strong point.

DIRECTION. 2. Most careful arrangements must be made for keeping direction in the attack. Successive landmarks must be chosen that can be easily recognised.

Distance from jumping off line to each strong point or trench forming the objective, must be known to all ranks.

Direction in which assaulting troops will be facing when the final objective is reached - i.e. North, South, East or West, - must be known to everyone.

Every Officer and as many N.C.O's as possible must be in possession of compasses and know the compass bearing of their objective.

HOSTILE COUNTER ATTACKS. 3. (a) Hostile Counter-attacks are certain to be made as soon as our troops have reached their objective.

(b) Troops must hold out against them <u>to the last and no one must retire under any circumstances.</u>

Should any individual or individuals retire troops behind them <u>must never under any conditions</u> conform to the retirement.

On the contrary they must advance and counter-counter-attack the enemy at once.

(c) Troops must be made to realise that experience has proved that troops who retire invariably suffer 3 or 4 times greater losses than troops who advance.

(d) Junior Commanders must keep their men in hand and no scattering in search of souvenirs must be allowed on any pretext. Every opportunity for re-forming troops as reserves for repelling counter-attacks must be made use of.

(e) Counter-counter-attacks must be delivered on the initiative of the Officer on the spot. Success depends on the intelligence, dash and initiative of Junior Commanders.

MOPPING UP. 4. Care must be taken that adequate moppers up are detailed from the rear platoons to mop up the captured area.

ACTION ON REACHING OBJECTIVE 5. The objective when gained must not be too thickly held. Formed bodies must be carefully placed in rear for counter-counter-attack.

The closest touch must be kept between O.C. counter-counter-attacking troops and the Commander in front line so that the former may have all arrangements made for a sudden move forward, which must be made on his own initiative.

BATTLE PATROLS. 6. As soon as the Objective is reached Battle Patrols will be pushed out to points of vantage where they can give early notice of the approach of any enemy counter-attack.

FLANKS. 7. Touch must be maintained with units on the right and left and no gaps must be left.

If any units are held up their advance must be assisted by fire against the flanks of the enemy opposing them.

All units must be prepared to form a defensive flank on reaching their objective if the troops on their flanks are checked and must make every endeavour to join up with

P.T.O.

– 2 –

troops on either flank should there be a gap when the objective is reached.

MACHINE AND LEWIS GUNS. 8. Every available Machine and Lewis gun must be brought up immediately the final objective is gained and the main defence of the newly captured area entrusted to them while the men are digging in.

These guns should be placed some distance in advance or in rear of the line to avoid shelling.

CONSOLI-DATION 9. Work on organising defences and on consolidation must be begun at once no matter how tired the men are. The enemy will take some little time to organise a strong counter-attack, and this time must be utilised to the utmost to get cover and prepare for the counter attack which is certain to come and which can be easily beaten off if the Machine Gun defence is organised at once and our trenches are prepared with energy.

REPORTS. 10. Send back reports on the Situation. Without such reports it is impossible for the Commanders behind to organise efficient Artillery support for the troops in front.

Early information, although it may appear of little value to the sender, may be a great factor of success.

DEVELOP-MENT OF RIFLE FIRE. 11. Ensure that men use their rifles.
It is essential that rifles be kept free from mud. Men must carry brushes to clean the breeches and bolts of their rifles & wire to clear the muzzle of mud as already instructed. Covers must be kept on rifles as long as possible.

It must be understood that Rifle fire invariably wins the day.

PRISONERS. 12. Prisoners captured should be sent back immediately. The tide of battle may turn and the Prisoners lost become a source of danger.

FORMING UP 13. Much of the success of any attack depends on the lines of the assaulting troops being square with the objective to be attacked.

Forming up lines for each platoon must be carefully marked by pegs and taped.

Failure to do his leads to loss of Direction which is fatal.

TOUCH BETWEEN UNITS. 14. When a unit advances touch must be kept with units in rear. This touch must be kept both by the units in advance and the units in rear. Commanders should meet and organise this touch before the battle.

Neglect of keeping this touch has lately resulted in failure.

DEALING WITH STRONG POINTS. 15. If some strong points hold on after our troops have passed them it is best to leave them alone until the attacking troops have securely established themselves beyond them and made themselves secure from counter-attack.

Then and not till then call on them to surrender.

ENEMY AEROPLANES. 16. Enemy aeroplanes flying low over our lines must be brought down by Lewis and Machine Gun Fire.

17. It must be remembered that it is a point of honour for every man in the 32nd Division that any position captured is held to the last and that not an inch of ground gained is ever given up.

Lieut-Colonel,
General Staff,
32nd Division.

28/11/17.

16th Highland Light Infantry

AMENDMENT TO OPERATION ORDER

Para. 14. of O.O. is cancelled and the following substituted :-

14. (1) Brigade Headquarters will be established at KRONPRINZ FARM with an advanced report centre at point 83 D.4.a.8.4. and VIRILE FARM (present Coy H.Q.)

   (2) The positions of Battalion Headquarters will be as follows:-

        No.1. Battalion MEETCHEELE - D.5.c.90.95
        No.2. Battalion BELLEVUE   - D.4.d.7.2.
        No.3. Battalion)
        No.4. Battalion) point 83 - D.4.a.8.4.
        No.5. Battalion PILL BOX at V.28.c.7.8.
        No.6. Battalion VIRILE FARM

   The Battalion Headquarters of the left Battalion of the 8th Division (2nd Rifle Brigade) will be at D.5.c.90.95. in the same PILL BOX as those of No.1. Battalion.

   (3) Battalions will also establish advanced Headquarters in the vicinity of our present front line.
    The 16th High. L. I. Battalion Headquarters will be at VOCATION FARM.

Reference last line of para 9 (Action of artillery) for "200 yards" substitute "300 yards".

                                           Captain & Adjutant,
    16th High. L. I.

30th November, 1917.

War Diary
of the
10th Battalion The Highland Light Infantry

Volume XXVII

From 1st to 31st January 1918.

Army Form C. 2118.

Vol 26

WAR DIARY
or
INTELLIGENCE SUMMARY.
(Erase heading not required.)

Volume XXVII   Page 1

Instructions regarding War Diaries and Intelligence Summaries are contained in F. S. Regs., Part II. and the Staff Manual respectively. Title pages will be prepared in manuscript.

Place	Date	Hour	Summary of Events and Information	Remarks and references to Appendices
LOUCHES	1918 January 1st		In Billets in LOUCHES. The Commander-in-Chief under authority granted by His Majesty the King has awarded the following Decorations:— **Distinguished Service Order** Lieut Colonel Robert Kyle **The Military Cross** Captain George Caulfield **Distinguished Conduct Medal** No.14784 Corporal Henry Kirk	weft
LOUCHES	2nd		In Billets in LOUCHES	weft
LOUCHES	3rd		In Billets in LOUCHES	weft 25.P 8weke

Volume XXVII Page 2

Army Form C. 2118.

WAR DIARY
or
INTELLIGENCE SUMMARY

(Erase heading not required.)

Instructions regarding War Diaries and Intelligence Summaries are contained in F. S. Regs., Part II. and the Staff Manual respectively. Title Pages will be prepared in manuscript.

Place	Date	Hour	Summary of Events and Information	Remarks and references to Appendices
LOUCHES	1919 January	4th	In Billets in LOUCHES. The undermentioned Officers joined the Battalion on this date. Captain R. M. Ballantyne Lieut. Sm. Lancroft 2/Lieut. B.M.N. Heddle 2/Lieut. W.J. Watson 2/Lieut. J.L. Young 2/Lieut. W. Murray 2/Lieut. B. McKinnon 2/Lieut. J.M. Williamson 2/Lieut. W.H. Reid 2/Lieut. R.M. Hardy	welft
LOUCHES		5th	In Billets in LOUCHES. Reinforcements of 111 o.r. joined the Battalion on this date	welft
LOUCHES		6th	In Billets in LOUCHES	welft

Army Form C. 2118.

WAR DIARY
or
INTELLIGENCE SUMMARY

(Erase heading not required.)

Volume XXVII Page 3

Instructions regarding War Diaries and Intelligence Summaries are contained in F. S. Regs., Part II. and the Staff Manual respectively. Title Pages will be prepared in manuscript.

Place	Date	Hour	Summary of Events and Information	Remarks and references to Appendices
LOUCHES	7th		In Billets in LOUCHES	welt
LOUCHES	8th		In Billets in LOUCHES. Reinforcements of 41 o.r. joined Battalion on this date	welt
LOUCHES	9th		In Billets in LOUCHES	welt
LOUCHES	10th		In Billets in LOUCHES	welt
LOUCHES	11th		In Billets in LOUCHES	welt

Volume XXVII Page 4

Army Form C. 2118.

WAR DIARY
or
INTELLIGENCE SUMMARY
(Erase heading not required.)

Place	Date	Hour	Summary of Events and Information	Remarks and references to Appendices
	1918 January			
LOUCHES	12th		In Billets in LOUCHES	w.e/t
LOUCHES	13th		In Billets in LOUCHES	w.e/t
LOUCHES	14th		In Billets in LOUCHES	w.e/t
LOUCHES	15th		In Billets in LOUCHES	w.e/t
LOUCHES	16th		In Billets in LOUCHES	w.e/t

Army Form C. 2118.

WAR DIARY
or
INTELLIGENCE SUMMARY
(Erase heading not required.)

Volume XXVII   Page 5

Instructions regarding War Diaries and Intelligence Summaries are contained in F. S. Regs., Part II. and the Staff Manual respectively. Title Pages will be prepared in manuscript.

Place	Date 1918 January	Hour	Summary of Events and Information	Remarks and references to Appendices
LOUCHES	17th		In Billets in LOUCHES	weft
LOUCHES	18th		In Billets in LOUCHES	weft
LOUCHES	19th		In Billets in LOUCHES	weft
LOUCHES	20th		In Billets in LOUCHES. The Battalion entrained at AUDRUICQ Railhead and detrained at ELVERDINGHE, and proceeded by march route to "P" Camp on POPERINGHE - WOESTEN ROAD)	weft
"P" Camp	21st		In Hutments in "P" Camp	weft

WAR DIARY or INTELLIGENCE SUMMARY

Volume XXVII Page 6

Army Form C. 2118.

Place	Date 1918 January	Hour	Summary of Events and Information	Remarks and references to Appendices
"P" Camp	22nd		In huts in "P" Camp	W3/7
"P" Camp	23rd		In huts in "P" Camp	W3/7
"P" Camp	24th		In huts in "P" Camp. Reinforcements of 78 or joined Battalion this date	W3/7
"P" Camp	25th		In huts in "P" Camp. The Battalion moved from "P" Camp to Billets at B.3.C.2.6., Sheet 28	W3/7
B.3.C.2.6.	26th		In Billets in DECORT AREA. The Battalion relieved the 10th Bn The Camerons in Support in HET SAS Right Subsector. Relief complete 6.30pm	W3/7

Army Form C. 2118.

Volume XXVII page 7

WAR DIARY
or
INTELLIGENCE SUMMARY
(Erase heading not required.)

Place	Date 1918 January	Hour	Summary of Events and Information	Remarks and references to Appendices
HET SAS	27th		In support HET SAS Sector. The Battalion relieved the 10th Black Watch in the Right Subsector. Relief complete.	welft
HET SAS	28th		In occupation of HET SAS Right Subsector. Casualties: 2 O.R. wounded by M.G. fire.	welft
HET SAS	29th		In occupation of HET SAS Right Subsector	welft
HET SAS	30th		In occupation of HET SAS Right Subsector	welft
HET SAS	31st		In occupation of HET SAS Right Subsector	welft

W.D. Scott
Major,
Commanding 16th High. L.I.

15/231.

To : "A"
   Headquarters,
      32nd Division.

      Herewith War Diary for the period 1st to 28th February, 1918.

                       a.macfarlane
                      Captain and Adjutant, for
        Lieut Col., Commanding, 16th High. L. I.

28th February, 1918.

To : D.A.G.,
　　　General Headquarters,
　　　　3rd Echelon.

　　　Herewith War Diary for the period 1st to 28th
February, 1918.

　　　　　　　　　　　　　　　　amacfarlane
　　　　　　　　　　　　　　Captain and Adjutant, for
　　　　　　　Lieut Col., Commanding, 16th High. L. I.

28th February, 1918.

Confidential

War Diary
of the
Highland Light Infantry
16th Battalion
Volume XXVIII

From 1st to 28th February, 1918.

Army Form C. 2118

Volume 28 Page 1

WAR DIARY
or
INTELLIGENCE SUMMARY

(Erase heading not required.)

Instructions regarding War Diaries and Intelligence Summaries are contained in F.S. Regs., Part II. and the Staff Manual respectively. Title Pages will be prepared in manuscript.

Place	Date 1918 Feby	Hour	Summary of Events and Information	Remarks and references to Appendices
HET SAS	1st		In occupation of HET SAS Right Subsector. The Battalion was relieved by the 5/6th Royal Scots and moved to BABOON CAMP. Relief complete 11.50pm.	—
BABOON CAMP	2nd		In hutments BABOON CAMP	—
BABOON CAMP	3rd		In hutments BABOON CAMP. The undermentioned Officers joined the Battalion on this date:— Lieut J. M. Whyte from 6th H.L.I. 2/Lieut F. Middlemiss Do 2/Lieut J. Templeton Do 2/Lieut J. Mann Do	—
BABOON CAMP	4th		In hutments BABOON CAMP. The Battalion relieved the 2nd Manchester Regt in Reserve in HET SAS Left Subsector. Relief complete 4pm.	—
HET SAS	5th		In Brigade Reserve HET SAS Left Subsector	—

WAR DIARY
or
INTELLIGENCE SUMMARY
(Erase heading not required.)

Army Form C. 2118

Volume 28 Page 2

Instructions regarding War Diaries and Intelligence Summaries are contained in F. S. Regs., Part II. and the Staff Manual respectively. Title Pages will be prepared in manuscript.

Place	Date 1918 Sept	Hour	Summary of Events and Information	Remarks and references to Appendices
HET SAS	6th		In Brigade Reserve HET SAS Left Subsector. The Battalion relieved the 17th High L.I. in HET SAS Right Support. Relief complete 10.30pm.	
HET SAS	7th		In Brigade Support HET SAS Right Subsector. The Battalion was relieved by 16th Lancashire Fusiliers and 2nd K.O.Y.L.I. and moved into Brigade Reserve. Relief complete 12.30 am.	
HET SAS	8th		In Brigade Reserve HET SAS Right Subsector. The Battalion relieved the 11th Border Regiment in HET SAS Sector Left Subsector. Relief complete 8.30pm.	
HET SAS	9th		In occupation of HET SAS Sector Left Subsector.	
HET SAS	10th		In occupation of HET SAS Sector Left Subsector. The undermentioned Officers from 17th High L.I. joined Battalion on this date:—
Major L.R. Paterson, M.C.
Adjutant J. Cathie
Lieut. R.M. Nelson
Lieutenants R.M. Thomson, I.D. Sinclair, R. Morrat, J.S.J. Brown, J.H.G. Mussen, A.M. Palmer, E. Baird, J. Riddle
Reinforcements of 150 o.r. from 17th High. L.I.

Casualties:— 1 o.r. Wounded (Died of Wounds) | |

WAR DIARY or INTELLIGENCE SUMMARY

Army Form C. 2118

Volume 21 Page 3

Place	Date 1918 June	Hour	Summary of Events and Information	Remarks and references to Appendices
HET SAS	11th		In occupation of HET SAS Left Subsector	any
HET SAS	12th		In occupation of HET SAS Left Subsector. Casualties 1. or. Missing	any
HET SAS	13th		In occupation of HET SAS Left Subsector. Reinforcements 4. or. joined Battalion this date.	any
HET SAS	14th		In occupation of HET SAS Left Subsector. The Battalion was relieved by 2nd. H.O.7.L.I. and proceeded to Brigade Reserve. Relief complete 9.30 pm. Casualties 1. or. wounded.	any
HET SAS	15th		In occupation of HET SAS Brigade Support	any
HET SAS	16th		In Brigade Support HET SAS	any
HET SAS	17th		In Brigade Support HET SAS	any

WAR DIARY
or
INTELLIGENCE SUMMARY.
(Erase heading not required.)

Army Form C. 2118.

Volume 28 Page 4

Instructions regarding War Diaries and Intelligence Summaries are contained in F. S. Regs., Part II. and the Staff Manual respectively. Title pages will be prepared in manuscript.

Place	Date	Hour	Summary of Events and Information	Remarks and references to Appendices
HET SAS	18th		In Brigade Support HET SAS	
HET SAS	19th		In Brigade Support HET SAS. 97th Infantry Brigade and noted as Divisional General Reserve Battalion. The Battalion was relieved by the 15th High. L.I. and moved to Huttments in BABOON CAMP. Relief complete 8.10pm.	
BABOON CAMP	20th		In Huttments BABOON CAMP. At 12 noon the 16th Highland Light Infantry was transferred from the 97th Infantry Brigade and posted as Divisional General Reserve Battalion. The reorganisation of Infantry Divisions which was undertaken at this time involved among other changes the selection of one Infantry Battalion in each Division for use as technical troops (Pioneers) under the C.R.E. The 16th Battalion Highland Light Infantry was selected to hold this place in the 32nd Division by reason of the uniformly high standard of working and fighting which it had attained during 27 months on the Western Front.	
BABOON CAMP	21st		In Huttments BABOON CAMP. Reinforcements of 40 o.r. joined Battalion on this date	

Volume 28 Page 5   Army Form C. 2118.

WAR DIARY
or
INTELLIGENCE SUMMARY.
(Erase heading not required.)

Place	Date	Hour	Summary of Events and Information	Remarks and references to Appendices
BABOON CAMP	22nd		In Authority BABOON CAMP. Battalion Headquarters moved to CANAL BANK. The reorganisation of the Battalion as a Pioneer Battalion of 3 companies was completed this day. Officers were posted as under :— *Headquarters* Lieutenant, R. Kyle D.S.O. Major Wm B. Tait S.S.O. M.G. Capt & Adjt J. Macfarland Capt. Q.M. R. Simpson. Lieutenant O.G.H. Stewart *"A" Company* Captain J.H. Reid Captain R.T. Martin Captain J.J. Cronin Lieutenant W. Gray Lieutenant St V. Childers Lieutenant H. Young D.C.M. M.M. Lieutenant J. Templeton Lieutenant J. McLellan M.C. Lieutenant R. Kay.	

Volume 78 Page 6

WAR DIARY
or
INTELLIGENCE SUMMARY.
(Erase heading not required.)

Army Form C. 2118.

Instructions regarding War Diaries and Intelligence Summaries are contained in F. S. Regs., Part II. and the Staff Manual respectively. Title pages will be prepared in manuscript.

Place	Date	Hour	Summary of Events and Information	Remarks and references to Appendices
BABOON CAMP	22nd		"A" Company (Cont'd)	
			2 Lieutenant R. M. Hardy	
			2 Lieutenant J. P. Mitchell	
			2 Lieutenant M. J. McInnes	
			2 Lieutenant F. Middlemiss	
			2 Lieutenant J. Thomson	
			2 Lieutenant J. R. Marrat	
			"B" Company:—	
			Captain A. Frew	
			Captain J. Catto	
			Lieutenant S. M. Roberts	
			Lieutenant J. Miller	
			2 Lieutenant R. Baird	
			2 Lieutenant D. Macfarl	
			2 Lieutenant A. M. Williamson	
			Lieutenant B. McKinnor	
			Lieutenant A. S. Sinclair	
			Lieutenant H. Murray	
			Lieutenant A. S. Gorans	
			Lieutenant R. M. Wilson	

Army Form C. 2118.

WAR DIARY
or
INTELLIGENCE SUMMARY.
(Erase heading not required.)

Volume 28 page 7.

Instructions regarding War Diaries and Intelligence Summaries are contained in F. S. Regs., Part II. and the Staff Manual respectively. Title pages will be prepared in manuscript.

Place	Date	Hour	Summary of Events and Information	Remarks and references to Appendices
	22nd		"B" Company (Con'td) Lieutenant R.H.L. Thomson Lieutenant D. Kiddie "C" Company Major P.R. L. Palmer, M.C. Captain H.E. Pawitt Foster A/Captain J.G. Harris Captain R.L.T. Ballantyne Lieutenant McMahon Lancaster Lieutenant J.W.E. Sherson Lieutenant J.W. White Lieutenant J. Mann Lieutenant H. Fingland Lieutenant S.M. Mabon Lieutenant W.H. Reid Lieutenant J.S.T. Brown Lieutenant A.V. Clark Lieutenant W.N. Heddle Lieutenant S.H. Smith Lieutenant R.B. Robertson	

WAR DIARY
or
INTELLIGENCE SUMMARY.
(Erase heading not required.)

Army Form C. 2118.

Volume 23 Page 8

Place	Date	Hour	Summary of Events and Information	Remarks and references to Appendices
	1917 23rd		"C" Company (Contd) 2/Lieutenant C.F.F. Edie Lieutenant R.B. Stewart Captain F.L. Ourr. Harris, S.O. Medical Officer The new position and duties of the Battalion were accepted with enthusiasm by all ranks.	
BABOON CAMP	23rd		In BABOON CAMP and CANAL BANK	
BABOON CAMP	24th		In BABOON CAMP and CANAL BANK	
BABOON CAMP	25th		In BABOON CAMP and CANAL BANK	
BABOON CAMP	26		In BABOON CAMP and CANAL BANK The Battalion moved to BOESIGHME CAMP.	

Volume 28 Page 9

WAR DIARY
or
INTELLIGENCE SUMMARY.
(Erase heading not required.)

Army Form C. 2118.

Place	Date 1918 Feby.	Hour	Summary of Events and Information	Remarks and references to Appendices
BOESIGHHE CAMP	27th		In hutments BOESIGHHE CAMP.	
BOESIGHHE CAMP	28th		In hutments BOESIGHHE CAMP. Under authority granted by His Majesty the King of the Belgians the Commander in Chief has awarded the following Belgian decoration:- Croix de Guerre No. 40505 Sergeant James Robertson No. 3475 Private Patrick Connachan No. 33130 Private William Chapple R. Chyle Lieut Colonel, Commanding 16 Highland Light Infantry	

To: D.A.G.,
   General Headquarters
      3rd Echelon

Herewith War Diary of the 16th (Service) Bn Highland Light Infantry for the period 1st to 30th April, 1917.

R Kyle
Lieut Colonel,
Commanding 16th High. L. I.

30th April. 1917.

Vol #17

17.P.
15 sheets

War Diary

of the

16th Battalion The Highland Light Infantry

Volume 18

From 1st to 30th April, 1917.

WAR DIARY
or
INTELLIGENCE SUMMARY.

(Erase heading not required.)

Army Form C. 2118.

Instructions regarding War Diaries and Intelligence Summaries are contained in F. S. Regs., Part II. and the Staff Manual respectively. Title pages will be prepared in manuscript.

Place	Date	Hour	Summary of Events and Information	Remarks and references to Appendices

OFFOY	30th		In Billets in Corps Reserve in OFFOY
			Brigade Inspection
			    The Battalion as part of the 97th Infantry Brigade was inspected by the G.O.C., 32nd Division on this date.
			
			    The Corps Commander under authority of His Majesty the King has conferred the Military Medal on the undernoted:- dated 26th April, 1917.
			
			    No. 14315 Corporal R. Wylie
			    No. 12095 Piper T. Richardson.
			
			                          Lieut Colonel,
			            Commanding, 16th Highland Light Infantry.	

Appendix 1.

16th (Service) Battalion H.L.I.

Congratulatory Messages received for

Operations of 14th April, 1917.

From Commander - in - Chief.

Please convey my congratulations to 32nd Division on the success of the operations carried out by them on 14th April, 1917.

From Army Commander.

General RAWLINSON wires as follows AAA Please convey to 32nd Division my best congratulations on the phenomenal success of their operations to-day AAA The vigour and gallantry of 32nd Division is worthy of high praise, and I offer them my warmest thanks AAA

From Corps Commanders

The Corps Commander desires his thanks to be conveyed to all ranks of 32nd Division together with his congratulations on their success.

From Divisional Commander.

The Divisional Commander wishes all ranks informed that the success of the Division is entirely due to the careful plans of Brigade Commanders coupled with the intelligence, rapid movement and great dash of the troops AAA The splendid support given by the Artillery enabled the Infantry to carry out their tasks without excessive casualties, and the determination and spirit shown by the 32nd Division to-day proves that it can go anywhere and do anything.

From Brigade Commander.

Well done, 16th H.L.I.

--------- : - : ---------

Appendix 2

16th (Service) Battalion H.L.I.

Preliminary Operation Order.

INFORMATION. The French intend to attack ST. QUENTIN at an early date.

They will capture ROUCOURT, FAUBOURG ST MARTIN, and if successful will push forward into suare T.7.

INTENTION. As soon as the French have taken the whole of their objectives the 97th Infantry Brigade will attack and capture FAYET, and its defences.

TROOPS EMPLOYED. This attack will be carried out by the 2nd K.O.Y.L.I. on the left and the 16th High.L.I. on the right, supported by the 97th M.G. Coy., 219th M.G. Coy., 97th T.M. Battery and all available Artillery.

ASSEMBLY POSITIONS.
The 2nd K.O.Y.L.I. will assemble on a line :-
Road bend (S.3.b.9.9.) to Cottages in (S.4.a.2.1.)
The 16th High.L.I. will assemble on a line :-
Cottages (S.4.a.2.1.) to Road (S.4.c.5.1.).

ORDERS TO TROOPS.
(a) Objectives.

The dividing line between assaulting Battalions will be a line from the cottages (S.4.a.2.1.) to FAYET CHATEAU (Road triangle S.5.a.8.8. and CHATEAU inclusive to 2nd K.O.Y.L.I.)
The first objective will be a N and S line drawn to FAYET CHATEAU.
The 2nd objective will be the sunken road running through squares M.36. and S.6. Ancn.Min. in M.36.a. inclusive, and the high ground to the North on a line M.35.a.0.6. to M.35.b.9.3.
(b) Method of Attack.
Assaulting Battalions. The 2nd K.O.Y.L.I. will attack the first objective with one Company astride the SELENCY-FAYET Road, and one Company down the hostile Trench running through suare M.34.

The left Company 2nd K.O.Y.L.I. will secure the Northern flank and take up a position facing N. about the junction of the German trench in M.34., and the FRESNOY - LE PETIT - FAYET Road.

The second objective will be attacked with two Companies, the left Company scuring the high ground to N. in M.35.
The left Company of the original assault will, simultaneously with the attack on the second objective, protect the left flank by exploiting success northwards along the hostile trench running through M.34.b. to M.35.b.9.6.

The 16th High.L.I. will capture the first objective with two Companies.
Theses Companies will consolidate a position on the southern outskirts of FAYET as soon as the second objective has been secured.
The second objective will similarily be attacked with two Companies, who will consolidate along the sunken road with the right flank slightly refused.

MACHINE GUNS.
The 219th M.G. Coy. will act under orders of O.C. 97th M.G. Coy.
Four sections will take up positions about the Copse in M.33. Central and cover the left flank of the attack. Fire will also be directed on the Ancn. Min.
Three Sections will take up positions about the

www.ingramcontent.com/pod-product-compliance
Lightning Source LLC
Chambersburg PA
CBHW080908230426
43664CB00016B/2754